M000204503

The Unlikely Duke

The Unlikely Duke

Memoirs of an eclectic life – from
rock 'n' roll to Badminton House

HARRY BEAUFORT

HODDER &
STOUGHTON

First published in Great Britain in 2023 by Hodder & Stoughton
An Hachette UK company

1

Copyright © Harry Beaufort 2023

The right of Harry Beaufort to be identified as the Author of the Work has been
asserted by him in accordance with the Copyright, Designs and Patents Act 1988.

All rights reserved. No part of this publication may be reproduced, stored
in a retrieval system, or transmitted, in any form or by any means without
the prior written permission of the publisher, nor be otherwise circulated
in any form of binding or cover other than that in which it is published and
without a similar condition being imposed on the subsequent purchaser.

A CIP catalogue record for this title is available from the British Library

Hardback ISBN 9781399725194
ebook ISBN 9781399725200

Typeset in Celeste by Hewer Text UK Ltd, Edinburgh
Printed and bound in Great Britain by Clays Ltd, Elcograf S.p.A.

Hodder & Stoughton policy is to use papers that are natural, renewable
and recyclable products and made from wood grown in sustainable
forests. The logging and manufacturing processes are expected to
conform to the environmental regulations of the country of origin.

Hodder & Stoughton Ltd
Carmelite House
50 Victoria Embankment
London EC4Y 0DZ

www.hodder.co.uk

To Georgia, without whose guidance and love I would
never have written this book

Author's Note

I hate upsetting people and I realise that some of the stories in this memoir inevitably reflect the attitudes of the time in which they took place and include language and views that are now rightly considered to be outdated and offensive. This material has been retained to convey the atmosphere of the time, and its inclusion does not mean that I condone it.

Contents

INTRODUCTION

Welcome to the Machine

MY FATHER ONCE mentioned to my sister Anne, an eminent historian, that she should follow the lead of Lady Gwendolen Cecil, who laboured over a four-volume biography of her father, the third Marquess of Salisbury. He expanded on the idea, suggesting that the subject of Anne's efforts should not be her father, but rather her brother – me. He then added, with typically understated wit, 'I fear it might be rather a slim volume.'

Of course, my lifetime achievements will never match those of Salisbury, who enjoyed three stints as Prime Minister at the height of Britain's Victorian splendour. Nonetheless, while inhabiting the slowly dying world of aristocratic privilege, I have also sought out friendships with people not normally associated with that milieu.

I am the 12th Duke of Beaufort. An unlikely heir, my father was the first cousin twice removed of the 10th Duke, inheriting the title and estate only because the 10th

Duke was childless. Unlikely also because, while my ancestors seemed to be mainly preoccupied with country sports, my interests lie with the worlds of music and popular culture, resulting in a life lived somewhat in contrast to previous generations. At times it has also been a life lived in contrast to the formal setting of Badminton House, where I now live. The late Queen and the Royal Family have been regular guests at Badminton, but rock royalty such as Mick Jagger and Eric Clapton have also stayed here.

This autobiographical project has circled in my mind for some time, but I have been prevented from setting pen to paper by the general laziness that has intermittently dominated my life. I've always kept a diary, and when Covid lockdowns hit, I found myself, like everyone, at home, no longer gallivanting around parties and other social occasions. I paced about and, with nothing else to do, ended up poring over my diaries, reliving much of my life. The idea of a book surfaced again at a time when there were no reasons to prevent writing it.

As I embark on this memoir, I am sitting at my desk at Badminton overlooking the deer park, where not much has changed since Canaletto painted it on his European Tour in 1748. The view is occasionally disrupted by events such as the Badminton Horse Trials, attended by 150,000 people every year, or by the film crews and wedding parties we increasingly rely on to help keep the wolf from the door.

CHAPTER 1

Champion Ice-Cream Eater

Wearing the sailor suit that I always wore to London tea parties.

MEMORY IS A strange beast. At least once a week I recall a boy by the name of Henry Shaw. I have not seen him since my private-school days; indeed I don't even know if he is still alive. But he once demonstrated to me a priceless skill: if you hold your arms up in the air when standing under a shower, the water encases your entire body, mimicking the feeling of lounging in a hot bath. Every time I now conduct a similar operation the name of Henry Shaw resurfaces in my mind. On the other hand, many events and people of considerably more significance have vanished into the mists.

Alongside my own unreliable memory, there is the memory of my family, dating back centuries. My nanny was the first person to inform me of my future duke potential. At this stage it was still uncertain whether or not my father would inherit the title of Duke of Beaufort, but that didn't stop me from quickly deciding to mark this territory

5

with my younger sister, rather boastfully demanding that she undertake some additional task for me on the grounds of my newly discovered seniority; I was subsequently severely reprimanded for this unattractive behaviour by my father.

The family is descended from John of Gaunt, son of Edward III and father of Henry IV. Gaunt was also a direct ancestor of Henry VII's mother Margaret Beaufort. Margaret's brother was the Duke of Somerset, whose illegitimate nephew, Charles, married a Welsh heiress called Baroness Herbert, the owner of large estates in Wales that included Raglan Castle. This union resulted in their family prospering through the Tudor era, and they were eventually given the Earldom of Worcester in 1514.

The 4th Earl of Worcester bought the manor of Badminton for his younger son, but by 1655 this branch of the family had petered out, so it reverted to the main family, and in particular to Lord Herbert, the eldest son. He was a figure of almost Machiavellian cunning: the family's Welsh lands had by now been confiscated by Oliver Cromwell due to their support for Charles I during the Civil War, but Herbert won himself back into favour by converting to Protestantism, and then grew progressively more friendly with Cromwell himself. Along the way he was wise enough to marry a rich widow and, after the Restoration of Charles II and flipping sides again, he was rewarded with the return of the bulk of the Welsh lands.

Herbert found himself one of the richest men in the land. Unfortunately, Raglan Castle had been destroyed during the Civil War, so the decision was made for the family to move to Badminton, where, shortly after their arrival, construction of Badminton House commenced. Herbert succeeded to his father's title in 1667 and then, ever closer to the King, was created Duke of Beaufort in 1682. It is thought he may have been the architect for the house as it is not attributed to anyone else, and he had a keen interest in architecture. He was even clever enough to recognise William of Orange as monarch in 1688 after the Glorious Revolution, despite having fought *against* him during the invasion.

The Beaufort family have been at Badminton ever since. Compared, for example, to the aforementioned Salisburys, the Dukes of Beaufort have wielded limited power on the national stage during this period of 350 years, but the estate in general has been sensibly managed and, mainly as a result of the aesthetic bent of the 3rd Duke, there are some fine works of art in its ownership.

When I was born in 1952, my parents lived in Eaton Terrace in Belgravia, so the first few years of life were in London. My father was an officer in the Coldstream Guards when he met my mother, Caroline, at a dinner party. It was an unusually hot night, and my mother said my father did nothing but complain about the heat, whereas she found the man sat on her other side (the ostensibly less glamorous David Rasch, who later married my father's sister Anne) totally charming. However, by the end of the night, somehow there was an undeniable chemistry between them. Something clicked, and soon they became a couple.

My mother Caroline Thynne was the only daughter of Henry Thynne and Daphne Fielding. Daphne was part of the Bright Young Things in the 1920s, friends with the likes of Evelyn Waugh, while Henry was set to inherit Longleat. When they announced their intention to marry, some moves were made by the respective families to end the engagement – too much madness on both sides was the fear. In defiance they insisted on getting married, but few would deny the eccentricity of the subsequent progeny, in particular Alexander, the late 7th Marquess of Bath, who became well known in the 1990s for painting large nude murals in Longleat and having a harem of women he described as 'wifelets'.

Daphne and Henry married in St Martin-in-the-Fields in 1927, subsequently becoming the sixth Marquess and Marchioness of Bath. They had five children, including my mother, who grew up at Longleat as her parents pioneered the stately home industry. The marriage ended in divorce in 1953 and Daphne began a new chapter of her life, becoming a popular society author, writing numerous biographies.

My father David Somerset was the second son of Bobby Somerset and Betty Malcolm. While his father (my grandfather) was the first cousin once removed of the 10th Duke of Beaufort, it was expected that the Duke would produce an heir of his own, so throughout my father's childhood he, and his elder brother Johnny, grew up without any idea of what the future held. When the Second World War began, my father was eleven and Johnny was fourteen. Both went to Eton, after which Johnny joined the Coldstream Guards, but he was killed in action when he was just twenty, in April 1945. The following year, when my father was eighteen, he too joined the Coldstream Guards. By now, with the 10th Duke nearly fifty and without an heir, it became clear that the line was set to go sideways to my grandfather, Bobby Somerset, and then, with Johnny having died, to my father.

My mother's family, the Baths, were a rich family, but they adhered to a total belief in male primogeniture, whereby the eldest son inherits everything and girls and younger sons virtually nothing. This was made worse for my mother and her siblings: they were bound by a clause in their trust as a precaution against extravagance, and so were not allowed to sell any of their stock, all of which comprised very low-yielding government bonds. My father was able to extract Caroline from this arrangement when they got married, and her money gradually grew into a respectable portfolio, but her brothers had to endure this situation for the rest of their lives. It was probably more important than my mother realised to make a good match, but she was uncomfortable with the courting rituals of debutante parties and later recalled having spent a lot of time as a wallflower, despite her unusual beauty.

When my father left the army in 1949 he ventured into business, becoming a partner of Marlborough Fine Art thanks to being blessed with a piece of luck; the artist Paul Maze, a friend of my grandfather, knew two Jewish art dealers, Frank Lloyd and Harry Fischer, who had escaped Nazi Germany and set up Marlborough Fine Art in England. They were looking for a partner who could make a small capital injection into their business and open doors to the great country houses, which at the time were shedding many masterpieces from their collections as the high-tax regime of the Attlee Labour government began to bite. Aged twenty, my father had a naturally aesthetic bent but a limited knowledge of art, so during his early assignments my mother had to whisper into his ear to remind him precisely which painting in the room he had come to see. Her knowledge was extensive despite her education having been regarded as of secondary importance compared to preparing her for a suitable marriage. Like many intelligent girls of her background, she read widely to educate herself, and became something of an expert in history and literature. I remember her telling me that, even though she was not religious, she had set herself the task of reading the Bible from cover to cover because she felt it was something she ought to have read.

Fortunately for my father, my mother's knowledge of art helped him in the early days of his new venture, and it did not take him long to develop a serious level of expertise. The partnership with Lloyd and Fischer went from strength to strength, helped along by my father's connections with people such as Gianni Agnelli of the Fiat dynasty. They had met in the south of France on my parents' honeymoon and at that stage of his life Agnelli was more the playboy than the successful industrialist he subsequently became, but he was able to introduce my father to some of the richest people in the world, many of them big players in the art market. Agnelli and my father – both possessed of a certain mysterious restlessness – struck up a lifelong friendship, partly sustained by a shared love of beautiful women. My father used to speak to Agnelli almost every day at six in the morning, much to the annoyance of my mother, who was not an early bird. Their friendship mainly evolved in glamorous Mediterranean locations, seldom accompanied by wives. I, in fact, met Agnelli only about ten times in my life.

I arrived less than two years after my parents wed. By the time of my birth, they were fully aware that my father stood in line to inherit Badminton, so when I was christened not only was the Duke one of the godparents, but so also was Queen Mary, widow of King George V, and aunt to the 10th Duke's wife. To this day I wear her present of gold cufflinks, engraved with my initials. She had been evacuated to Badminton during the war and was, at her request, made a godmother. Born in 1867, she was eighty-five at the time and died a year later.

There was still an element of austerity in the air, with rationing only completely ending in 1954, and a vaguely grey feeling hanging over the 1950s. Despite this, my parents and their friends did their best to recreate a bygone era, perhaps clinging on to everything they knew in the wake of so much change and uncertainty. Firmly keeping to tradition, an upper-class wife was not expected to work, but would hand over a huge degree of responsibility for her children to a nanny.

Nanny Nelson looked after me and my younger sister Anne, who even at this early age had been christened Monster by the family because, when she was very young, she had rather unruly hair that kept falling over her face. My father's mother, in consequence, started calling her Gorilla, and this later evolved into Monster.

Nanny Nelson remained in post until I was seven. We adored her, but with hindsight our daily routine of seeing our mother for only an hour at the most after breakfast, and then after tea, seems quite strange, not least because my Mother spent much of her time downstairs playing patience and compiling rather obscure lists. When later she showed us these lists, her full eccentricity was revealed. One was headed 'People Who Might Be Murderers', and included Greek shipping tycoon Stavros Niarchos, whose wife died mysteriously, and Claus von Bülow, who was tried for but eventually acquitted of murdering his wife in a notorious trial in the 1980s. She also listed people she knew who had been murdered, but this group tended to comprise obscure characters such as Mrs Muriel Mckay, who was mistakenly kidnapped in 1969 in the belief that she was Rupert Murdoch's wife; poor Muriel used to exchange greetings with my mother when they were seated next to each other at the hairdresser. The kidnappers were the first to be convicted of murder without a body, as Muriel was never found. On a more mundane note, the lists included the heading 'Things to Do', in which the first entry was 'Go for a walk', the second, 'Watch television', although I doubt she consulted these entries every time she was at a loose end.

But even had she wanted to be more present as a mother it would have been difficult: the slightest intrusion on to Nanny's territory resulted in an immediate threat to leave, a misery our mother was reluctant to impose. At the time this was the norm and therefore accepted, but I'm sure my mother would have preferred not to have her life and her relationship with her children dictated by the nanny. For nannies, though, their job was their entire life. In the 1960s, a nanny's leisure time was limited to one afternoon off a week. It was therefore not surprising that most of them never married, as they rarely had the opportunity to meet men. This, perhaps, made them all the more proprietorial of their charges and it must have been a recurring sadness when the children eventually grew out of the nursery and the nanny had to move on.

In some ways Monster and I lived a sort of double life,

divided between the cosy existence of time in the nursery and being extracted – sometimes unwillingly – to join our parents for weekends away. Once, for my fifth birthday, I had two parties on consecutive days, one for the children looked after by Nanny's friends and one for children whose parents were friends of my mother. I went to a lot of children's parties and adored being generally boisterous.

Hyde Park was our principal playtime location. For this excursion we were dressed up in ridiculously smart clothes, which inevitably got dirty very quickly, especially for a rather unathletic boy like myself, who fell over a lot when playing any game. I developed a way of dealing with this, often falling over on purpose just for the sake of laughs. I remember being chided quite angrily by my mother when I took yet another fall. '*Do* stop doing the falling-over joke,' she complained wearily. I did eventually graduate to more mature areas of humour, although sometimes I look back with a wistful envy at such easy routes to making people laugh.

Often, we were marched to Miss Ballantine's dancing class, in a studio just off Sloane Street. I don't actually remember being taught any dancing, so I assume it was just an excuse to play games such as musical bumps, at which, due to my falling-over specialisation, I proved particularly proficient.

I am not sure whether it was these unnecessary demonstrations of clumsiness, or something else, but Nanny Nelson became totally determined that I was a delicate boy who would benefit from a visit to the most famous paediatrician of the time. My mother was reluctant to agree, but, after considerable difficulty, got the appointment. She then suffered the indignity of some very strong words from the doctor, berating her for wasting his valuable time by bringing a perfectly healthy boy to the clinic.

I showed limited signs of any great ambition even at this age. I recently unearthed a press cutting in which my mother and two of her friends were accosted by a journalist in the park and the three children were asked what they wanted to do when they grew up. The others produced the fairly standard answers of soldier and train driver, but I selected the more unusual choice of 'champion ice-cream eater'.

As I got a little older, the contrasts between life with Nanny, and life with my parents, became starker, illustrated on our annual holidays with my father's parents, Bobby and Betty, who, from the 1950s onwards, were based in Majorca. Bobby was an adventurer, spending much of his time indulging in his principal hobby of sailing, racing his most famous yacht, the *Jolie Brise*, all over the world. He would have been aware – theoretically – that he was heir to the Duke of Beaufort if the 10th Duke failed to have children, but they were roughly the same age and I suspect it rarely crossed his mind.

The holidays were fun; the vibe, compared to being looked after by Nanny Nelson at home, entirely more relaxed. While we loved Nanny, time with our parents revealed areas of activity where they had more to offer. Nanny maintained a strict line on vulgarity, with various punishments threatened if we overstepped the mark. Not so our parents, particularly my father, who could not resist this easy route into our affections. On occasion it was difficult to gauge how far we could go. Once, at home in London, I was surprised at the lack of audience success when he came up to the nursery after a hard day at the office and I stood up in the bath and demonstrated my pissing skills.

I brushed off Nanny's chiding after this offence and have retained a love of vulgarity to this day, albeit displaying it in subtler and less explicit ways. In this respect there were exciting new territories to conquer on holiday with Nanny left behind: I discovered the joy in hearing my parents swear. It was obviously something mildly taboo, but for reasons I couldn't pinpoint. Monster and I did little else on that holiday other than experiment with various exciting expletives. In turn, this forced our parents to adopt a rather strange scale of (pre-decimalisation) fines: 'Hell' 2 pennies, 'Damn' 5 pennies, 'Bugger' 8 pennies (perhaps cheap at the price in today's climate), 'Bloody' 10 pennies and finally 'Fuck', a full shilling.

My grandfather, Bobby, had a certain boyish charm about him and was adored by my father, who referred to him as 'The Oracle', because of his practical but rather vague wisdom. Once, Betty made an urgent request that, when guests were aboard his yacht, he should go on deck if he was about to fart. This made total sense to Bobby, so he climbed the steps and poked out his head before releasing the offending smell; the only problem being that he was now aiming directly into their faces.

When Bobby's mother died, she romantically requested in her will that her ashes be taken out to sea and blown wherever the four winds should take them. His vagueness once again came to the fore and he climbed into a rowing boat in a rather dirty harbour, went out about fifty yards and tipped them over the edge, before proudly returning to land, believing he had fulfilled her wishes. While we only saw Bobby and Betty once a year on holiday, Bobby had made efforts with me, showing me his various skills, teaching me how to use a penknife and how to fire a catapult.

It came as a huge shock when Bobby tragically drowned in 1965 while sailing in a storm off Rhodes. He, along with his crew, had been on deck when they hit the rocks; the crew and one guest were able to jump clear, but Bobby went down to try to save the women sleeping below, alas in vain. When his body was recovered his arms were clamped across his chest, and my grandmother liked to believe he had found his beloved dog Jessica and was trying to carry her to safety.

My father was telephoned at home with the news. My mother later told me it was all rather uncomfortable as he sobbed uncontrollably in front of the servants. Bobby was only sixty-seven when he drowned, but my father always reflected that he wouldn't have enjoyed the limitations that growing old would have placed on his boyish enthusiasms.

It was the second time in my father's life that he had prematurely lost a close member of his family, following his older brother, Johnny's, death in the war. He later told me that, during his brief flirtation with adulthood, Johnny had become incredibly extravagant, throwing lavish dinner parties, and, while my grandparents were concerned at the time, it gave them some small comfort to know that he had at least enjoyed these moments of hedonism.

When Bobby died, my father was in his late thirties, so, unexpectedly early, he became the heir apparent to the dukedom.

CHAPTER 2

Master

Master riding with the Queen and Princess Margaret at Badminton.

BADMINTON HAS 116 rooms. A guest once decided to measure the distance from their bedroom to the billiard room, and declared it was about an eighth of a mile. The walls are covered in paintings, most of which are family portraits, from Tudor ancestors to a Graham Sutherland painting of my maternal grandfather and a large photographic portrait of my father.

Although the house looks vast from the outside, the west wing is almost entirely given over to public events. But I am fortunate to live in some of the nicest rooms, where my parents created a cosy environment amid the seventeenth-century Grinling Gibbons carvings, the ornate Thomas Willement wallpaper and the Great Staircase, designed by Sir Jeffry Wyatville for the 6th Duke. A huge mirror hangs at the bottom of these stairs, a potential health and safety nightmare for guests who cannot help admiring themselves as they come downstairs in their evening clothes.

The North Hall, which faces on to the park, was where the game of Badminton was invented in 1863. Its chequered floor marks out the proportions of a badminton court. On the walls hang large paintings by John Wootton, one of the great equestrian artists of the early eighteenth century, who began life as a page and was sent by the 3rd Duke to Rome, where he perfected his artistic skills. Wootton's paintings in the North Hall mainly depict hunting scenes, for which he was best known, but the most striking is the one above the fireplace. It shows Grey Barb, a horse imported by the 3rd Duke and supposedly one of the five Arabs that all thoroughbreds are descended from. This may not be quite right, however, as I was once told that, unfortunately, Grey Barb was infertile.

During my childhood, Badminton was dominated by one individual: the 10th Duke of Beaufort, who lived there for sixty years. An imposing man, he was known by his nickname, Master, due to his absolute devotion to fox-hunting, which for years he carried out six days a week, being dubbed 'the greatest fox-hunter of the twentieth century'. As Duke of Beaufort, he was Master of the Beaufort Hunt, but he was also Master of the Horse, by royal appointment. He came from a long line of huntsman and his father was completely obsessed likewise. On the day Master was born (christened Henry) there was a meet at Badminton and a huntsman suggested marking the occasion with 'three cheers'. His father, the 9th Duke, said no on account of not wanting to upset the hounds.

At Eton great things were predicted for Master as he exhibited both academic and sporting prowess. Having just missed the First World War, he did a short stint in the army and then decided to devote his life to a traditional aristocratic country existence. He loved being outside and rode around the grounds every morning without fail. At the retirement dinner of Charlie, the head forester, his exact contemporary, Master made a speech. He described how when they were children he would stand at the end of the wood while Charlie clawed his way through the brambles, rousting up the birds to fly over him to shoot, and concluded the speech by saying, 'And by God we had fun, didn't we Charlie?'

Within his chosen framework Master was extremely successful: very much a pillar of the community and generally highly respected, as well as being a good friend of the Queen. They shared an equal love of horses, always together at various annual horse events. The link was closer still through his wife, who was a member of the Royal Family. Born Princess Mary of Teck, she was the daughter of Prince Adolphus of Teck, whose older sister was Queen Mary. In 1917, on account of the First World War, German titles within the Royal Family were replaced with new British ones, so her father became Marquess of Cambridge, and she was known as Lady Mary Cambridge until she married Master. Like him, she loved riding, cutting an elegant figure riding side-saddle through the park.

When I was five, it was proposed that Monster and I should move to Badminton to live in a nursery wing of the house. This decision was made when Master had bonded with, and developed sufficient faith in, my father to create the Somerset Trust, a vehicle by which the Badminton estate could be passed on to the next duke on his death. This was more difficult than might be believed, as there were clauses in his mother's will that were advantageous to her relations and had to be bypassed with certain financial inducements.

Master's life was almost exclusively country based, while my father inhabited a racier and more sophisticated world; nevertheless, a bond slowly grew between them, and my father had a great respect for Master. I think this was always a controlling feature in the back of my father's mind, stopping him doing anything too reckless.

We were accompanied by Nanny Nelson at Badminton. My father still had to work in London, so my parents came down only at weekends and stayed in London during the week. This was quite a change: no longer an endless stream of other children to play with. Luckily, Nanny had a real liking for the countryside and slotted easily into the new life. Monster and I relied on her to compensate for our relative lack of playmates, as she was quite creative, and from this period I acquired some lifelong interests.

She loved watching National Hunt racing on television, something my parents did not enjoy, and I quickly became encyclopaedic on the subject. This led me to develop a rather

strange hobby whereby I adapted a set of about thirty colour-
ing pencils into horses, each with a different name, and
flicked them into something resembling a gallop. I accompanied it with manic commentary, which was diverting enough
that my parents insisted their relatively talentless son
exhibit his skill to assembled crowds. I also liked to construct
a show-jumping course by putting two bamboo sticks into
the ground, with a further one placed horizontally across
them, using clothes pegs as a support. I would prance about
in the manner of a horse and jump the fences, with any
fence knocked down penalising me four faults. I became so
obsessed with this activity that my father told me later he
had briefly worried I actually thought I was a horse.

Master and Mary had lived alone in Badminton since
1924, apart from when Queen Mary was evacuated to live
there during the war, so it must have been strange for them
to have to share the house. It was very sad for Mary that she
could not have children, as they would have been central to
everything that happened, or was planned for, at Badminton.
Her main compensation for this was to always have about
ten dogs, which she took on rampaging walks every day,
often asking me to accompany her.

Mary treated me as an informal grandson, and with my
parents usually in London she suggested I come down to
dinner every evening in my dressing gown. This was not
exactly the treat it was intended to be. Master and Mary
always sat in the huge formal dining room, which was dark

and often very cold. As conversation at dinner inevitably revolved around dogs or hunting, the alternative – television in the nursery – was considerably more attractive. The food was disgusting, and menus were ruled by the calendar: in the shooting season we constantly ate very dry pheasant, or, when the deer were being culled, repulsive slabs of venison weighed heavy on the plates. Master was totally uninterested in food and, although he had the facility of a wine cellar, he did not appear to drink anything other than the small jug of orange squash by his place at every meal.

Sitting uncomfortably eating unappetising dinners with Master and Mary was possibly a better alternative than if Master's father, the 9th Duke, had been there. In his old age the 9th Duke used to be strapped into his chair by the fire in the great hall at Badminton every day after dinner. He would then immediately fall asleep, leaving the assembled servants with the unenviable task of waking him up when it was time to go to his bed, whereupon he would thrash out at the nearest person as hard as he could with a stick. Bobby Somerset went to stay there as a boy and described him as 'the nearest thing to an animal I've ever met'.

My father told me of one breakfast when everyone was quietly absorbed leafing through the papers, except for Master, who always used this time to read his post. Suddenly peace was shattered as Master roared down the table, 'Does anyone know what *masturbation* means?' There followed sheepish silence and suppressed giggles. Mary squawked back from the other end, 'I think it's something to do with the hound puppies, Master.' Everyone remained bewildered how this rather strange conversation had begun, and it turned out that Master had been written to by some man asking him to lend the weight of his position to the creation of a National Day of Masturbation.

Master's chosen lifestyle did rather shield him from the outside world. After the war the Beaufort Hunt was looking for a new joint master and an application came through from India, admittedly in slightly illegible handwriting, from a certain Major Gundry, who was serving in the army there. Delighted by this interest, Master urgently contacted the hunt committee with the news that Mahatma Gandhi had applied for the job, in no way surprised that the great visionary was considering such a drastic career change.

By spending time with Mary, I discovered some interesting aspects of her character, one of which was that she harboured a pathological hatred of Germans. In some ways this was quite surprising as, by dint of being a niece of Queen Mary, she was half-German herself. Despite this, on the rare occasions when any German came to the house, she was quite unashamed to display her xenophobia in the form of a rather eccentric rudeness.

She was equally inflexible on the political front and horrified when my parents introduced her to a friend, the very soft-left Labour MP Woodrow Wyatt (who later became a trusted confidant of Margaret Thatcher). The mere fact of his being affiliated to that political party made him *persona non grata* at Badminton.

On another occasion during an election campaign, she was riding home from hunting and saw that a junior maid from the house had had the audacity to display a Labour sticker in the window of her cottage. Mary leapt off her horse, rang the doorbell and furiously insisted she tear it down *immediately*. This dictatorial behaviour did not cause any lasting disaffection and the maid rose to become the housekeeper in later years.

Master had similar run-ins around the grounds, perhaps because he had been brought up in an era when, at least within the square miles around the Badminton estate, he could believe in some sort of 'divine right of dukes'. One day my father was out riding with him, and they reached a gate that was jammed on its hinges, and neither of them could open it without dismounting. Master noticed a man carrying out some maintenance work up a telegraph pole in the road beyond the troublesome gate, and respectfully asked if he would oblige. The man either did not hear this request or did not see why he should accede to it. This prompted a total change of mood in Master, and he bellowed at full volume, 'Open the bloody gate, damn you!' The shocked man shimmied down the telegraph pole like a fireman summoned to an urgent call and carried out the requisite task, after which Master reluctantly thanked him and carried on with the ride, seeing nothing unusual in the exchange.

In the relatively small world of hunting Master was something of a celebrity, people being fascinated by even the most mundane aspects of his life. My father was once out shooting and one of the guests came up to him after the first drive with the rather surprising question: 'What does Master have for breakfast?' My father furnished the unsurprising reply of 'Eggs, bacon and sausage,' and assumed the conversation was over. However, after the next drive the man approached again and continued probing: 'So, he likes a sausage, does he?' It was all my father could do not to prolong the discussion for the rest of the day.

In the winter Master spent much of his time in pursuit of the fox, but in summer he liked nothing more than spending hours watching the young fox cubs through his binoculars as they frolicked around. On one occasion a huge dog appeared and scared the cubs away, in his mind a very serious offence indeed. He became even more angry when he discovered that the dog belonged to the architectural historian and writer James Lees-Milne, and his wife Alvilde, who at my father's suggestion had recently become tenants of one of the houses in the village. Master had been a bit doubtful about this as Lees-Milne, although one of the great diarists of the age, was not exactly the rugged sort of man who normally constituted his circle of friends, and he now felt his suspicions had been confirmed. Still furious, he stormed round to the Lees-Milne house, shotgun in the crook of his arm, and, despite receiving some sort of apology for the dog's solecism, he couldn't resist a parting shot, 'You don't hunt, you don't shoot, what *do* you do?'

Master showed a similar lack of understanding when he went to stay with his friend the Duke of Northumberland, whose son and heir Harry Percy was suffering from serious mental health issues. Master could see that things were not quite right with the boy but couldn't quite put his finger on why. On his return to Badminton he commented, 'Poor Hughie Northumberland has terrible problems with his boy. He's given up hunting.'

More than a decade after he died, Master would have been appalled when the Labour government promised to abolish fox-hunting. While I have never loved it like Master, I have maintained a strong support for the sport as an integral part of country life that no metropolitan elite have the right to interfere with. I used to take my own children out in the car on a cold winter's afternoon, waiting by a wood in the hope of catching a glimpse of the hunt. When they crested the brow of a hill, the hounds in full cry, I would always feel the scene was a thing of beauty and that we must do everything in our power to fight any ban, so I joined the Countryside Rally. In 1998, a year later, I attended the Countryside March, where in excess of four hundred thousand country people descended on London to protest against the proposed ban, and there was a wonderful feeling of camaraderie on both occasions. Tony Blair admitted in his autobiography that, had he known the feelings the ban would engender, he would never have embarked on it.

The most enjoyable occasion was the demonstration outside parliament about five years later. By then the ban was about to become law and there were some angry people about. These were not so much hunting toffs, who are sometimes wrongly portrayed as the only people involved in fox-hunting, but more 'deep country' people who really resented the threat to their way of life, and there was palpable aggression in the air against the lines of policemen and the government photographers working alongside them taking pictures for their records.

I became emboldened among these chanting groups and was right at the front when scuffles began breaking out. Swept along in the fleeing crowd as the police responded, I couldn't resist feeling mildly proud the next day when the journalist Charles Moore observed in his description of these scenes how 'the towering figure of the Marquess of Worcester' was at the centre of the foray.

The demonstration was the lead on the evening news, not least because Otis Ferry – the son of the musician Bryan Ferry – and other pro-hunt activists had managed to invade the chamber of the House of Commons, a security breach that had not been achieved for nearly four hundred years. As a result of this, when the countryside community went down to Brighton a few weeks later to demonstrate outside the Labour Party Conference, the police presence was so strong that it was impossible to make an impact of any kind. Instead, a group of us gave up and enjoyed a large lunch at one of Brighton's excellent fish restaurants.

The ban on hunting did eventually become law, but it was drafted in such a way that hunts are still able to operate subject to some very strict rules, and I think the fact that these were not more draconian was because by this time Tony Blair's principal aim was to try to kick the problem under the carpet.

While most hunting people continued to indulge in the sport in this modified way, the one person who could not risk being seen doing so was Prince Charles, who, prior to the ban, had hunted with the Beaufort whenever he had the opportunity. There was no doubt where he stood on the subject and he sometimes attended fundraising evenings that some of our local farmers organised, with the West Country comedian Jethro as star attraction.

Jethro did not appear on television for the simple reason that his act would have no chance of passing the censors – it was incredibly vulgar. His jokes were scatological, one involving him accidentally having sex with his mother-in-law – but he was a genuine comedy great with the most perfect timing and facial expressions. At Badminton he was capable of sending a barnful of around two thousand people into complete hysterics, and the person who seemed to enjoy his act the most was Prince Charles, who on one occasion was laughing so much I was worried that he was going to have a heart attack. The Royal Family have a famously ribald sense of humour and my mother once told me that she was present when her friend Anne Tree told an extremely rude joke to the King of Greece, who, incidentally, loved it. When my mother questioned the wisdom of telling such a joke, Anne replied, 'I just wanted to check that he was royal.'

Fortunately for Master, hunting remained intact for the duration of his life. I fear I was something of a disappointment to him, particularly in relation to this obsession. One day I happened to be in exactly the spot where the hounds killed the fox. Shortly afterwards Master rode round the corner and, seeing me there, fired the question, '*Which hound killed that fox, Harry?*' This would have been a tough one even for a hunting obsessive and I couldn't muster a better answer than 'I don't know,' which provoked a vague look of disdain at this lack of what he regarded as standard general knowledge.

Cub hunting was the (now illegal) early-season way of teaching young hounds their trade by the riders surrounding a wood and not allowing a fox to escape the chasing pack. One early cub-hunting morning I was riding a very difficult horse that did not enjoy this discipline and simply would not stand still, going round and round and then lunging forward to eat grass, all of which was totally exhausting. Eventually, in desperation, I turned the horse from the wood and, miracle of miracles, a feeling of total peace enveloped the animal, probably because it was no longer watching the hunting action. Unfortunately, at this precise moment Master rounded the edge of the wood and deduced that I was a complete halfwit facing the wrong direction. Cue another bellow of the familiar refrain, 'You bloody fool!'

While Master was disappointed by my lack of natural interest in hunting as a child, my parents were concerned about my friendship with Jed, the butler's son. On arrival at Badminton our social life was saved by the fact that Master and Mary, despite entertaining fairly modestly, still employed a mini army of butlers and footmen. The head butler was called Mr Abbott, but my parents quickly became aware that, like many others in his profession, he had succumbed to the delights of the wine cellar and regularly stumbled and swayed when serving dinner. As a non-drinker, Master was not familiar with these symptoms and simply complained about how clumsy he was. Eventually the problem could be concealed no longer, and Abbott was sacked.

This meant that the under-butler, Leslie Vacher, could step into his shoes, having waited some twenty years for this promotion. Leslie had five children, the fourth of whom was Jeremy, or Jed as we quickly started to call him, who was the same age as me. Nanny Nelson soon incorporated him into our orbit as a regular playmate. Such friendships were prevalent in many upper-class families but tended to peter out when the privileged boy went off to boarding school. However, Jed remained a close friend until he emigrated to Australia after leaving school. I revelled in the delights of seeing Jed, building camps in the woods, buying sweets in the village shop and rushing around the grounds. My parents were not at all in favour of this friendship, thinking Jed's wild village ways a bad influence. But my friendship with him was both formative and enjoyable and the scrapes we got into over the years turned what could have been a rather monotonous childhood at Badminton into something much more exciting.

CHAPTER 3

Bunter

With my father and three siblings in 1970.

EVER SINCE INFANCY and the days running riot with Jed, I have always loved watching television. Apart from sleeping, television is something I devote more time to than anything else. In my entry in *Who's Who* I list 'selective television watching' as one of my hobbies, and scouring the weekend newspapers planning what to watch next week is a pleasure that goes on giving.

I inherited some of my extreme enthusiasm for the medium from my mother, who acquired one of the earliest video recorders in the 1970s when I was in my early twenties. This was something of a luxury at the time, and Monster and I were reliant on her to record programmes such as *Upstairs, Downstairs* or *I, Claudius* to watch when we came down from London for the weekend. Unfortunately, her technological skills were often found wanting and I can remember on more than one occasion sitting down in anticipation, only to be greeted by her accidental recording of *Tomorrow's World*.

Eventually the science of recording became simpler, and this coincided with the advent of the golden age of television that continues today. The main beneficiary of this was series television, allowing for character development over a longer period, and since the Millennium there has been a holy trinity of shows that epitomise this: *The Sopranos*, *The Wire* and *Breaking Bad*.

When I was a child growing up in the 1950s, television was not twenty-four hours, so I would stare desperately at the test card waiting for *Watch with Mother* to start. When I was a bit older, there was *Garry Halliday*, a pilot who battled a criminal mastermind called 'The Voice', and above all the adventures of Billy Bunter, the greedy and extremely fat schoolboy, who I identified with so closely that my father started calling me Bunter. The nickname has stuck to the present day.

Some might think this a little cruel, but at the same time my sister Anne was christened 'Monster', a name that has also stayed with her, so I think it fair to say as a family we found unusual ways of expressing affection.

I also loved music and was given a record player for my sixth birthday. I would listen for hours to my favourite song, 'The Runaway Train', one of the four 78 rpm discs included with the present. However, the discovery of Bill Haley's 'Rock Around the Clock' quickly took me in another direction: rock music became a soundtrack to my life and remains so today. Rather unusually for a boy of six, I became a regular subscriber to the *NME*, or *New Musical Express* as it was known in those days. It wasn't so much the articles that attracted me, but a fascination with the charts and the various lists and statistics entailed within them. Some of these are still imprinted in my memory, despite their having to compete with other reading matter such as Enid Blyton's 'Famous Five' stories and the *Buster* comic.

In between these pleasures I started going to school, where I must have been rather a wet boy. Early on, a class-mate pointed a toy revolver at me, saying, 'Stick 'em up,' to which I could only reply, 'Stick *what* up?'

In 1960, when I was nearly eight, it was decided we should return to London. I think this was instigated by Nanny Nelson, who thought I would be better prepared for boarding school (looming six months in the future) at the fashionable day school Hill House than at Grittleton, the local school near Badminton. In fact, having been pretty much at the bottom of the class in the country, in London I found myself, if anything, ahead of the pack, so my derided rural education must have been better than thought.

I still lacked social skills and, not for the first or last time in my life, television came to the rescue. I loved a programme on children's television called *Bonehead*, about a gang of totally useless criminals, of whom the most useless was Bonehead himself. Bonehead had a tendency to say either 'yeah boss' or 'sorry boss' in a half-witted way and, while I didn't need to be Laurence Olivier to imitate this, it hadn't been done before by any other boy, and so my whole class would dissolve into hysterics whenever I dipped into character. This proved an enormous confidence boost, and I began to experiment with other lines of humour and suddenly realised I could be funny, a gift I hope I have never lost.

Back in London, Nanny Nelson planned to resume the routines she had adopted when we were last there, seriously limiting parental access and threatening to leave if she didn't get her way. By this time, my brother Eddie had been born and my parents had grown in confidence and called her bluff. It was agreed she would leave for good while we were on holiday with them. Devastated, I cried myself to sleep.

With a new nanny in post who was much more involved with Monster and Eddie, I was allowed back to Badminton for the weekend with my parents, where I soon got over Nanny Nelson's absence. I would wake up at dawn, sneak down the back stairs and wander into the village and the country beyond. I had never been out of the house at that time of day before and loved the smell of the cold autumnal air and feeling of complete independence. I would always return in time for breakfast, and I am not sure anyone ever found out about my excursions.

While I enjoyed independence on my terms, the idea of boarding school filled me with dread. When the grim day dawned, my parents drove me, and en route they got totally lost. I nurtured the hope that, just perhaps, they would *never* find the school, and we could drive around together forever. Finally, though, they turned into a drive, and at the end loomed a rather magnificent building, of similar size to Badminton: Hawtreys School. Here I was to spend much of the next four years of my life.

The historian Lord David Cecil once commented that it was totally extraordinary how the English upper classes entrusted the care of their children, with virtually no restraints, to schoolmasters with whom they could barely face the thought of having tea.

There is no doubt it was an odd system, but I was a gregarious boy and in the main enjoyed my prep-school experience, although when I saw my youngest brother Johnson, twelve years my junior, sent off at a similar age, I was struck by how incredibly young he was to undergo such an experience. There were some boys totally unsuited to the regime, and they suffered a miserable time.

The first couple of weeks proved difficult, but once again my skills as a joker came to the fore and my popularity rose. The main problem was that, until Nanny Nelson left, I had been virtually dressed by her every morning and certainly had absolutely no idea how to make a bed. I had partially brushed up on these skills in the three months between her departure and my arrival at boarding school, but it still tended to be a slow process, and, as unpunctuality was punished by the loss of the sweet ration, I endured a sugar-free diet in my first term.

The headmaster of the school was called Mr Docker, and he ran it with his wife Phyllis, who sported a handlebar moustache. Many years later came rumours that they were, in fact, brother and sister, and that their pretence of marriage was purely to generate an element of respectability. Docker was generally fairly popular and ran the school well, but he was a believer in corporal punishment. All boys had to take communal showers after sport and there were always several with fearsome bruises displayed on their buttocks. I think we accepted this as part and parcel of school life, but I must admit I was one of the few boys who never suffered this indignity – I wasn't exactly a habitual offender but still think I must have been very lucky as well.

One day I committed some minor offence and was told to report to Docker's study after breakfast. Also waiting there was a boy who had been caught sliding down the bannisters on the stairs in the main hall, a cardinal sin as it could have resulted in serious injury. He went into the study first and from outside the door I heard some angry shouting and then the command to bend over, following which he received six very powerful strokes of the cane, interspersed with his screams. He then emerged crying, followed quickly by a visibly agitated Docker, who was breathing incredibly fast and heaving in post-orgasmic exhaustion, although at the time I interpreted this simply as excessive zeal from a headmaster carrying out his duty. Luckily, he was so exercised that he was totally uninterested in my own misdemeanour and screamed, 'Get out of my sight!'

Even worse was the case of the Latin master Mr Frewen who also taught at the school. From my point of view, he was probably the best teacher in the school, and the only unusual act he carried out on me was sticking his hand up the back of my shorts when I was standing at his desk having my work marked. I was vaguely aware this was unusual behaviour for a teacher, but I found it akin to a rather pleasurable massage, albeit, for me at least, totally non-sexual.

There were other tell-tale signs. Some boys used to go up to Mr Frewen's room for extra tuition, whereupon a sign was put on the door, 'Recording in Progress. Do not Enter' – I dread to think what that signified. We wondered why he was the only master who was never on duty for post-football showers, which now begs the question as to whether there might have been some complaint in the past that had been pushed under the carpet.

Even the relatively normal masters were an odd bunch. The PT coach was a monstrously ugly man known as Sergeant Major, or Sarge, who for all his rough ways we rather adored. He definitely favoured boys with superior athletic skills, a club of which I was very much not a member. On my first day I lined up behind the other boys to jump the 'horse'. After watching the rest of the class nimbly popping over it, I charged up not quite knowing what to do, and my apprehension proved correct as I somehow failed to take off and crashed into it. 'You're a useless ornament,' barked Sarge.

The hideous French teacher Mr Rappaport, nicknamed Rat, was undistinguished, but had a dog called Sir Barker, who occasionally accompanied him to morning break. Without fail it went totally berserk, charging around the extensive grounds chased by every boy at the school. In our ordered existence it was a wonderful outbreak of sheer chaos, and in the background, we could hear Rat screaming again and again, 'Sir Barker, come here, dog!' There was something extra amusing about the way he felt it necessary to add the word 'dog'.

Not surprisingly, the best thing about boarding school was the anticipation of coming home for the holidays. End of summer term was marked by a cricket match between masters and boys, after which the normal structures of lessons and school rules were relaxed. My excitement was undimmed by the fact that my parents were particularly bad at picking me up from school, and on one occasion forgot to turn up at all. Once back at Badminton, I would reunite with Jed and embrace the relative freedom of life with my parents, quite *laissez-faire* when it came to discipline. My parents were both smokers, and I could not resist testing whether the activity was quite as enjoyable as it looked. Egged on by the omnipresent Jed, I can still remember the thrill of stealing a packet of their cigarettes and smoking them in the garden. I inevitably spluttered a bit, but eventually mastered the skill. Monster, however, only about five at the time, dissolved into a serious coughing fit and was nearly sick. From that day she has never touched another cigarette, and I always say she has me to thank.

My brother Eddie must have watched me smoking and developed a similar fascination. When he was five years old, he found a box of my father's cigars and decided to experiment as to whether they were indeed as enjoyable as cigarettes. The trouble was that he had yet to realise that a cigar must be *cut* before smoking. Unperturbed, he duly worked his way through the box, chucking away each useless cigar when it failed to light, and in today's money wasting around £600. When discovered, there followed an element of displeasure from my father, but Eddie, ever the master of an improbable excuse, claimed it was the cat that had done it.

I was and remain extremely fond of Monster, but at the same time I was also rather a bully in the way I treated her in our childhood days. I cunningly announced that she could join 'the gang' with Jed and me, but only in the official capacity of 'gang slave', which meant she had to obey any order we gave. For a time, she gratefully complied with this edict and remained no less devoted for all its impositions. She has always maintained this level of loyalty: my father once quizzed her as to who would win in a tennis match between me and John McEnroe. 'Well, Bunter hasn't had so much practice,' came her reply.

Maybe we were particularly close because we didn't have

many other children to play with. When my own children were of a similar age, they were constantly being ferried to various tea parties. Back in my day, and perhaps because our nannies didn't drive, our social life remained more limited. The only outsiders we saw were two brothers, Burghie and Harry Fane, whose grandmother lived nearby, but the moment they arrived Jed and I immediately found it necessary to mark our territories by spending the duration of their visit fighting, so social engagement was limited in the early days of our friendship. Eventually they were permitted to join 'the gang', which, of course, increased the workload for the gang slave.

Most of the time though, it was just me and Jed. We'd ride our bikes through the servants' dining room and go off into the grounds and mess about. Once, we sat fishing for perch in the duck pond by the house, and Jed got up to fetch something, leaving his rod hanging over the edge of the pond. At this point came a fearsome noise of his reel being unwound, and suddenly the whole fishing rod was jerked from the bank and dragged round and round the pond. I screamed myself hoarse in excitement. We had never landed anything much over minnow size before, and now it seemed we had chanced upon a monster of the deep. The rod and huge fish on the end could be recovered only when my father was summoned and donned his waders. The unlucky fish turned out to be a large carp, and for many years thereafter it was spoken of in awed tones as 'The Big Devil'.

The highlight of the year was the children's fancy dress party, just after Christmas. The party centred around the ballroom, where various dancing took place, probably waltz based, but my principal memory is of charging aimlessly around the house making a huge amount of noise. Planning the costumes was exciting enough, but in addition Jed and I would decide to victimise some unfortunate guest, and we even allowed Monster a special dispensation to join in the nastiness. On one occasion we landed on my friend and contemporary George Kershaw as our target, but when we attacked, he proved so strong that body after body could be seen being thrown out of the scrum and we were obliged to retreat with tails between legs. It was perhaps no coincidence that, at every subsequent party until we were teenagers, George, who later became one of my greatest friends, always appeared in a suit of armour.

Scrapes with Jed were a constant during those years. Once, I found him throwing stones at a window – what an enjoyable activity, I thought. After we had both successfully cracked the glass, Jed picked up something more like a small rock, which inevitably achieved the intended result of smashing it to smithereens. Unfortunately, we hadn't realised our target was the back window of Badminton stables and, had there been a horse inside, we could have caused serious injury. Such behaviour was akin to blasphemy for Master, and I recall a creeping terror setting in as he marched up to our nursery to bellow at me. Punishments inevitably followed, one being that I was not allowed to come down to dinner for the rest of the school holidays, which of course meant I could enjoy the pleasures of television in the nursery as opposed to stilted dining room conversation. Much more draconian, though, was a ban from seeing Jed for the rest of the summer.

Back at school, I, along with the other boys, did somehow manage to engineer many freedoms, especially in the huge grounds where we could roam. We were also allowed to have radios, which gave at least some contact with the outside world. During the 1962 Cuban Missile Crisis older boys walked around, transistors pressed against their ears, whispering conspiratorially that the planet was about to be destroyed by nuclear war, although at the time I couldn't quite understand why. The following year I was eleven and by then had a keener interest in current affairs. I vividly remember the desk I was sitting at when Mr Frewen walked into the classroom and gravely told me President Kennedy had been assassinated, and I later made a scrap book of all the newspaper cuttings reporting his death and the aftermath.

As time passed, the main educational purpose of being at school loomed closer, namely passing the entrance examination to Eton. As a middle-ranking student, I was expected to achieve this, but in fact only just scraped in. Nonetheless, this was still an objective attained and on hearing the good news I hurled myself across a slippery wooden floor and crashed into the wall by way of an expression of delight.

Before leaving the school, every boy was summoned in their dressing gowns to Mr Docker's private quarters for the 'leavers talk'. This included discussion of whether we had had any thoughts about a future career, but also some outline information on the taboo subject of sex, about which we probably knew rather less than any boasting might indicate. Mr Docker included a brief mention of the temptations of the penis, with a rather stern command of, 'Whatever you do you must never touch yourself there.'

In a slightly emotional state about leaving a school I loved, I made a mental note to try to conform to this instruction. When I reached home, however, my father decided that he too should have a sex discussion with me. My mother later told me that he had whisked himself up into quite a stir over this task and got uncharacteristically drunk in anticipation. That may have encouraged him in the line he took, vigorously stating that one must *never* listen to schoolmasters on the subject, and that masturbation was in fact wholly natural. I was delighted by this clarification and celebrated in my bedroom for several hours afterwards.

*

When I was eleven, my parents moved into The Cottage, a fairly substantial house in the village that belied its name. It had previously been occupied by an elderly woman called Mrs Stanley, but there was an understanding with Master that, when she died, my parents could move in. By this time my father was making quite a lot of money as an art dealer and so building works, including the construction of a swimming pool, commenced. When we moved in, there was a wonderfully fresh smell about the place, as well as a general feeling of comfort not evident in the austere surrounds of Badminton.

There was also a huge improvement in the standard of food thanks to a Spanish couple my mother employed at The Cottage, who cooked delicious meals. The food was good enough to ignore the husband, Celso's, temperamental character. He regularly bawled at me and Monster for even minor infractions. They later emigrated to Australia, where Celso got into some sort of fight and was killed. On receipt of this news my mother rushed to her desk and extracted her book of lists: a new name to add to the list of people she knew who had been murdered.

The only downside of the move was that my parents decreed that Jed was not allowed into the house, in a new desperate attempt to wean me from his influence. We were, however, given an outbuilding in which some very scruffy furniture was placed, and we quickly christened it 'The Camp'. There was a wonderful feeling of it being totally our own. In subsequent years we painted it very unprofessionally from top to bottom and covered the walls with posters of Jimi Hendrix and The Beatles that we had bought in Carnaby Street. They looked down on us as we lolled about in useless teenager mode.

For many years the limited conversations I had managed with adults were invariably preceded by a single question: 'When are you going to Eton?' It was therefore a relief that I had passed as it was assumed that someone of my background would go there, and it would have been something of a failure not to achieve this. (Back then about 80 per cent of the boys there were sons of old Etonians; now the figure is closer to 20 per cent.) Arriving at Eton was something of an adventure, not least because we were allowed to visit the shops in the town. I was given pocket money of £5, meant to last the whole term, but I found the school tuck shops totally irresistible and had to send an SOS for emergency funds after only two weeks.

Chips and ice cream were my staples, and such was my greed that I used to run to the tuck shop in the mid-morning break, so that I had time to consume a plate of egg and chips, followed immediately by two additional plates of chips. On one occasion anticipation trumped timekeeping, and I charged towards the shop not realising there was actually another lesson to go before the break. I was unlucky to round a corner, going at full speed, and crash into my housemaster, knocking his books aside. He couldn't get his head around why, when I was meant to be studying in a classroom, I was careering for no obvious reason towards the town centre; I think initially he put it down to some desperate escape attempt.

My daily food intake became gargantuan: to start, a large, cooked breakfast, accompanied by porridge and a bread roll. This was followed by the aforementioned three portions of mid-morning chips, and then lunch a couple of hours later. If there were no sports, I would return to the tuck shop and have a couple of ice creams and then back to my house for 'boys' tea', which comprised food that we had either bought or had sent from home, and then, after two more hours, a cooked supper. I had arrived at the school a rather skinny boy but after a couple of terms I put on at least two stone and my weight-conscious parents became quite insistent that I alter my habits.

Some high achievers say the root of their success traces back to a particularly inspiring schoolmaster. This could certainly not be said of my housemaster, Jack Anderson, a rather unimaginative man who played everything totally by the book. He was, however, scrupulously fair, and I also credit him for being an early pioneer of Eton heading towards a ban on senior boys administering corporal punishment to juniors.

My best friend at Eton quickly became George Kershaw, or 'Kershaw' as even his wife still insists on referring to him, and a principal basis for this friendship was a shared enjoyment of the physical act of laughter, the quality of the preceding joke being of secondary importance. Every boy at Eton had their own room and ours happened to be directly one above the other. When we were lying in bed in the summer, it was rather enjoyable to shout some remark out of the window and roar with laughter, even if it wasn't particularly funny, but on hearing the echo of recipient laughter the trigger was pulled for an eruption of mutual hysterics.

One joke in particular sent this dynamic careering out of control. We conceived the idea of a rather fat master, called Guildford, suddenly coming through my ceiling, crashing through my floor into Kershaw's room and then on through his floor and landing in a giant bowl of jelly. The slapstick humour proved funny enough to send our laughter to ridiculous levels. Unfortunately, Kershaw's room happened to be directly outside Jack Anderson's study. Jack was sitting at his desk marking some homework and, disturbed by the cacophony, marched next door to silence Kershaw.

By the next morning the situation had become clearer, and Kershaw and I were summoned separately to Jack's study and punished with a full weekend weeding the garden. A humourless man, Jack couldn't really understand the basis of our behaviour, but suddenly displayed a more human side when he confided to me, 'I will say one thing, Harry, I am slightly relieved that you were involved in this as well, as I thought that boy Kershaw was having a fit.' On reflection I suppose anyone who just lay in bed alone bellowing with laughter might well be diagnosed with some form of insanity.

Kershaw had less pocket money than me but was always very generous, and on his mother's birthday we set off together to buy her a present. We entered a pharmacy and he announced to the shop assistant he wanted to buy some scent. She pulled out some bottles, but it quickly became apparent these were beyond his budget. As we prepared to leave, she added, 'But we do have some very nice toilet water.' I can still picture the look of incredulous surprise on Kershaw's face as he repeated the words 'Toilet water?', thinking she might be about to scoop this cheaper alternative out of the lavatory. After a few seconds he regained his composure but by this time I had collapsed on the floor in a fit of uncontrollable laughter.

In the summer term one had to choose whether to be a dry or wet bob, which meant cricket or rowing. In my first year I selected cricket because of my love of the game, but sadly lack of talent meant I rarely made the team, so the next year I took up rowing. I certainly showed no more skills at this discipline, but Kershaw and I absolutely adored rowing up the river on a summer's day to an island where you were allowed to order a limited amount of beer. We would then climb back into our boats suitably refreshed and deliberately capsize on the way home and flounder around laughing. I suppose this was the teenage equivalent of the falling-over joke that I had so enjoyed as a young boy.

My first two years at Eton were good but, lacking any sporting prowess and being disinclined to join any of the huge range of societies on offer, I found myself increasingly bored and was drawn towards a rather slobbish teenage rebellion. The main outlet for this was smoking, and almost every day I used to walk to Windsor with a boy called Burdett and go to a café, where we chain-smoked about four or five cigarettes. I don't think I particularly enjoyed this indulgence but there was a risk-taking pleasure and a joy at generally sticking a finger up at school rules.

Burdett and I then discovered Social Service, a charitable activity where boys from the school went to the hospital in Slough and helped look after patients. I quickly realised a career in medicine was not for me, but the advantage of this scheme was that on the way back we could go to a pub to drink and smoke before returning in a rather saintly manner to school and informing our housemaster of the good works performed. Unfortunately, our stays in the pub grew longer and longer and Jack grew suspicious and rang the hospital to discover that we had left several hours earlier. We were lucky not to get severely beaten.

By now we were very much on the offenders' register and our crimes finally came to an end when we were caught smoking again by an irritatingly cunning master who couldn't believe we were walking by a railway line purely for the pleasure of fresh air and exercise, and so stalked us and caught us red-handed. This time I was certain we would be beaten, but for some reason we got away with a Georgic (500 lines), though with an absolutely final warning that if we were caught again we would definitely be sacked. With only one term to go until A levels we thought it prudent to desist from such activities, but any sort of love affair I had had with the school was definitely over.

The last school holiday before schooldays were over for good was spent in the usual way of lounging about with Jed, while my mother gently encouraged me to revise for my exams. She spent most of her time in the country, with my father coming down for weekends and some of the school holidays. This gave her more time to be with my youngest brother Johnson, but the endless stream of affairs my father conducted may also have affected her decision. Although Johnson was twelve years younger than me, I quickly grew very close to him, and this bond has lasted throughout my life. I was also very fond of Eddie, but from an early age he always seemed to be in trouble, for things such as burning down one of the outbuildings to The Cottage, and also for pouring the contents of his potty on to Monster while she slept peacefully.

Although I was now a teenager, I too was still not immune from childish stupidities. There was an old Mini of my parents' that we were allowed to drive in the woods, where in the summer a team of Girl Guides used to camp. Driving past them on one occasion, with Jed in the passenger seat and Eddie in the back, Eddie chucked out some torn-up bits of paper, which fluttered down like confetti on to their campsite. Written on the scraps were minor obscenities such as 'fuck me pillocks' and 'have a shit'. Unfortunately, it happened to be parents' visiting day at the camp and, on reading these messages, one furious father leapt into his car and began chasing us. Such was his rage that he drove straight over a hedge by the wood, and I can still recall the sight of his car in mid-air in the rear-view mirror, and the simultaneous feeling that the shit had hit the fan. I can't quite recall if Eddie had committed this offence on his own or not, but I suspect he had been encouraged by me. Whatever the case, I was quite rightly the one blamed. I was interviewed by the police and once again my punishment was a period of banishment from the dastardly company of Jed.

This ban should have helped me focus for my A levels, but revision was not my strong suit. My attitude to academic work may have been framed by the fact that my father had a thing against universities. He had not gone himself, and his business career flourished in spite of that, so he couldn't really see the point of it. Perhaps he had read about the student riots in Paris in 1968 and thought it best that his son not be exposed to such temptation. I could, of course, have put my foot down and insisted on going, but the idea of never having to do another exam again held strong appeal. I therefore cruised towards my A levels with no ambition other than to pass them, which I did without much distinction. Not going to university has become one of my few regrets. Most other boys were full of exciting plans, and I remember one of them coming up to me and asking what I was going to do. I replied I intended to go to France and generally bum around but, as he went away looking a little confused, I felt a slight alarm. I had absolutely no idea what an honest answer to his question could have been.

Thirty years later, at an Eton reunion dinner, I was placed next to a man who had been in my house, and midway through the evening a fossilised memory came to the surface: I recalled that he laboured under the unique disability of inevitably farting whenever anyone hit him. Throughout the meal I had to squash a temptation to give him a jovial punch to see if he still retained this skill. I discovered I had been remembered in a particular way too when another old classmate came up to and said, 'You're the chap who used to use turquoise ink and accidentally set the plastic dustbin lid on fire.'

CHAPTER 4

The Hooray Years

A summer's day at The Cottage with my father.

ON LEAVING SCHOOL, I was wide eyed at the prospect of my future, but unsure which direction I wanted to go in. That summer of '69, Monster and I sat up until four o'clock to watch the moon landings. The original live pictures of the 'giant leap for mankind' were actually of appalling quality (they were doctored a few days later), so it was slightly less spectacular than might be thought, but it was still a phenomenal concept as we looked up at the moon. Less than ten years earlier such an achievement would have seemed like science fiction. For a young man about to embark on life in the real world it provided a rather wonderful feeling: anything was indeed possible. At the same time, though, came the apprehension that, were the technology and power that had got *Apollo* there harnessed in the wrong way, things could go spectacularly wrong.

One minute at school and the next supposedly an adult, my whole life stretching ahead, I still felt like a boy. Spending the summer holidays exactly as I would have done had I still been at school, as term time began and my siblings returned to school, I was aware of a certain void. Thinking it might be a good opportunity to broaden my horizons, my parents organised for me to live on a vineyard in France for a year with the Godepski family, who were friends of my maternal grandmother, Daphne Fielding. Since divorcing Henry Bath, Daphne had married Xan Fielding, a war hero fourteen years her junior, and exchanged the luxuries of Longleat for a bohemian literary life that had taken her to Cornwall, Tangier, Portugal and finally to Uzes in southern France. There she befriended mainly artistic types including the Godepskis.

The Godepskis were a very nice family, but I was bored and found the language difficult. Whenever any member of the family went to do something, I was sent with them, and these trips included riding western style in the Camargue and bullfights, or 'courses' as they were known, where the object is to pull a ribbon off the bull's horns rather than kill it, prizes being awarded to the bravest 'raseteurs' and the best bull. Rich men paid big prices for the most fearsome animals, rather as they would for a quality racehorse, and then entered them again at the next tournament.

Sometimes I'd spend the weekends with Daphne and Xan. When she first wrote her autobiography, Daphne had embarked on the project as a bit of fun, but now writing formed an essential part of her income and she had written a number of successful biographies of characters such as Rosa Lewis (later made into the television series *The Duchess of Duke Street*) and Emerald and Nancy Cunard. Xan was bilingual and earned his money as a translator, and they lived fairly modestly in a house by a single-track railway line, where the train drivers used to hoot at Daphne every time they drove past her garden, and she in turn blew kisses madly back.

Daphne and Xan had some interesting local friends including Lawrence Durrell, Dirk Bogarde and the sculptress Elisabeth Frink. I rather disgraced myself when, taken to a dinner party given by Lawrence Durrell, I displayed a certain inexperience about my capacity for drink. Durrell, who seemed quite keen on the substance himself, shouted rather woozily across the table, 'Drink! The boy must be allowed to drink!'

It was only a few years after this that Xan left Daphne for a younger woman. There was some concern about what would happen with her now that she was in her seventies. However, she quickly took up with an octogenarian American millionaire, and they lived very happily together until his death. When they came to stay at The Cottage, my mother asked rather cautiously if they would be sharing a bed. Daphne replied furiously to her daughter, 'Of course. Not only that but we'll be having sex as well.'

My timetable in France still revolved around the English school term at home, and I would return to coincide with half term and school holidays. Before leaving for France, I had been sitting in the nursery with my younger brothers when my father came in and rather casually handed me a document to sign, saying something like, 'Here are those army papers I was talking about.' I duly obeyed this instruction and found myself able to join the Coldstream Guards, his former regiment, on a short service commission should I choose to do so a year hence. I had virtually forgotten about this but, on one of my trips home, we started to discuss my future plans. My father eagerly reminded me of the opportunity, suggesting strongly it would be a good solution to my current lack of direction. It wasn't that he had any great attachment to the army, but he believed he had benefited from his stint of National Service after the war and felt it would do the same for me. The difference, of course, was that in his time it was compulsory, and he found himself among friends, whereas by the 1970s it was very much a certain type of person who joined the army and I tended to have little in common with such people. I also had a total allergy to the concept of any regime that required a short-back-and-sides haircut. I had no alternative suggestions but was adamant that this was not a path I wished to follow and refused point blank to go along with the idea.

Any decision was shelved. Instead, I opted to complete my time in France in Paris. The Godepskis had a contact there, Madame de Beaumont, who made her living by having foreign students living in her house in the fashionable Rue du Bac. What I had not realised, until arriving, was that all of her lodgers were girls.

When my father heard this news, he was rather excited and enquired optimistically, 'Good God. Are you stuffing all of them?' – but I was still shy and naïve and would have struggled to achieve such rampant success. I did, however, have a wonderful time living there and the girls seemed to like taking me under their wing; I talked for hours with them, enjoying their company. Through Gianni Agnelli my father arranged an internship for me at the advertising giant Publicis. In retrospect I think that advertising would have suited me, but at the time I did not show much enthusiasm for the job and my attitude worsened when all the girls I shared the house with suddenly disappeared home at the end of their university terms. Without my harem I decided to return home slightly early, although even now when I return to Paris, I feel embraced by that memory of 'Paris in the spring'.

Reluctantly, I enrolled for a six-month internship at Sebag's stockbrokers. It seemed a sensible plan to arm myself with a general grasp of the business world, but I don't think I have ever been so bored. Luckily my stay there coincided with a lengthy postal strike, so I was sent out every day in my car to deliver the post to all parts of London, and, with music blaring, this was infinitely preferable to sitting in a dull office twiddling my thumbs.

I had assumed I would be living in my parents' house, but

my father rented me a one-bedroom flat in Bayswater, possibly feeling my presence in his home would cramp his style. Harry Fane's brother, Burghie, from my childhood days in Gloucestershire, lived close by, lodging in Tim Hanbury's flat. Tim and I subsequently struck up a great friendship. Through Tim I built a social life in London, and my pursuit of hedonism blossomed.

The Hanbury family were originally brewers and at the turn of the century among the richest in the country. Tim's father James, however, was a monumental gambler. By the time he died all that was left from a colossal fortune was the remains of what had been a vast estate and a now rundown stately home, Burley on the Hill in Rutland, the majority of which was left to Tim's older brother, Joss. Their father did not have great business acumen and had sold much of the land that eventually became Milton Keynes because 'it didn't hold a fox'.

I used to go and stay at Burley, and it was great fun having the run of this huge house without any form of parental control. We played a fearsome variation of hockey in the ballroom, an accident waiting to happen, and the game was prohibited when one guest had his teeth knocked out. Despite inheriting only a small part of the estate, Tim was fortunate to have a selection of aunts and grandmothers who left him enough money to live very well in London, and perhaps having wealth as a young man encouraged him in an unusually wild lifestyle.

On one occasion Tim was stopped by the police for driving on the pavement to overtake a dawdling car. He happened to have a bottle of whisky in the car and, as the policeman tapped on his window, he ostentatiously drank most of it. He was then breathalysed; unsurprisingly, he failed. When the case came to court, he claimed that he had not actually been drunk while driving but had consumed the bottle of whisky because he was so unnerved by the sight of the police. In his proof of this, the court was told how he had spent the evening in a casino where he had lost £2,000, and all sorts of waiters and croupiers were summoned to say that he had not been drinking during this time; miraculously, 'the hip flask defence', as it is now referred to in legal terminology, was accepted and he was acquitted of drink driving.

Unfortunately, he had also been charged with dangerous driving for the swerve along the pavement and this was more difficult to disprove. The judge, annoyed to be outwitted by a smart lawyer, announced that it was pointless to issue just the standard fine for this offence as it would be as nothing to someone of Tim's obvious wealth. He therefore gave Tim a two-year suspended jail sentence. This would have placed all sorts of limitations on Tim's future, so he appealed, and this time won, the court ruling that the sentence was unfair as all men should be equal under the law. For years afterwards law students had to study the case law precedent of 'Regina *v.* Hanbury, The Case of the Affluent Offender'.

As with most members of my generation, drugs occasionally accompanied alcohol. It is a slight myth that the swinging Sixties was the era when people started taking drugs, as, from memory, it wasn't until the 1970s that drugs really hit the mainstream. My first experience was with marijuana through the great comic actor Peter Sellers, who invited me to try it when I was a teenager. I knew him through the Mancroft girls, who were friends from Badminton, the eldest, Miranda, going on to marry him. He was very obliging when we asked him to do his Goon imitations, but the real moment of excitement came when he promised to give us some marijuana, which none of us had ever tried. Monster, me and our friend Harry Fane gathered at the Mancroft house in the country and, once the parents had gone to bed, Sellers passed the joint around. We smoked tentatively at first, glancing nervously at each other to see if there had been any reaction, and then somebody let out a sort of giggle, which had the instant effect of triggering mass hysterics in us all. While this was going on, Sellers sat on the sofa sphinx-like. I'm not sure if he had even partaken himself, but he certainly acted more in the manner of someone conducting an interesting social experiment, and eventually retired to bed leaving us to happily relive the experience.

Talking about drugs in a memoir is always a bit of a risk, as any media interest tends to try to upgrade it into some sort of 'my drugs Hell' story. This would certainly be unfair in my case as I never suffered from what could remotely be described as a problem, but there was a period of a few years when I took rather more cocaine than ideal. Cocaine gave me the confidence to overcome the shyness I felt towards anyone older than me, and after a line or two I found my charm seemed to be working universally. The feeling of invincibility was hard to resist. The reality, of course, is that cocaine turns you into rather a bore: you blabber along mindlessly, and it also keeps you awake, which makes for late nights and increased alcohol consumption.

Around this time, I became friends with Taki Theodoracopulos, who came from a rich family of Greek shipowners and is sixteen years older than me. If you tried to define a 'playboy', Taki would come as close as anyone to the model, inhabiting a world of money, beautiful women and fast living. He was originally a friend of Gianni Agnelli and my father, who both also enjoyed his boundless energy and the fact that, whenever he turns up, the action tends to follow.

He has chronicled this lifestyle in his weekly column in the *Spectator* for over forty years, and also wrote the book *Nothing to Declare* about his time in Pentonville Prison, following his arrest for smuggling a small quantity of cocaine into the country, which gives a salutary lesson in just how unpleasant it would be to spend even a short time in jail. When we met, he was married to the beautiful but long-suffering Alexandra, or 'the mother of my children' as he insists on calling her so as not to give even a small hint of his unavailability to potential conquests, although deep inside he is very fond of her. Taki's politics are definitely on the right end of the spectrum, and in discussion he certainly prefers to transmit rather than receive, with all his friends familiar with being shouted down by his conversation-stopping cry of, 'May I speak, may I speak!' He is blithe about causing offence, but for people he likes he maintains a code of honour and a deep loyalty.

Meanwhile, my brother Eddie got in with a bad crowd, most of them ending up with serious addiction problems. He was unlucky in that he left school and moved to London at the same time as heroin seemed to be a normal feature among privileged people of his age. Eddie, however, had the presence of mind to escape by taking up an offer from an Australian called Peter Jansen to drive one of his fleet of trucks, based in Melbourne. He returned six months later in very good health and cured.

My father was eternally grateful to Jansen, and the next time he was in England asked him to stay at The Cottage, and from then on, he became a regular, often staying over the Christmas period. Jansen thrived on playing the hard-drinking Australian to the full, and many late nights passed listening to his stories, inevitably extremely vulgar, laced with bad language but, when one was in the mood, incredibly funny. Jansen was a more than capable horseman, so my father lent him a horse every weekend to go hunting. He also rather enjoyed taking Jansen round to meet some of the grander locals. Once, we all went to have a drink with Lady Westmorland, mother of Harry Fane, who had, in her middle age, developed a slightly grand manner. When she was introduced to Jansen, I instantly noted a certain distaste in her attitude towards him as she asked, 'Hello Peter. Tell me, what do you do?' In his heavy Australian accent, he shot back, 'I just stick my little red sausage into as many holes as I can.' Not surprisingly, she recoiled in horror, muttering, 'Charming,' before storming away. I did detect in my father a sly amusement at the chaos created.

There are people close to me who have ruined their lives because of drugs and even died from using heroin, so I am aware of the potential problems, but alcohol, too, can take a heavy toll. For me, nowadays, the moderate use of cannabis has been at times, a genuine life enhancer, giving me the ability to encourage laughter, think originally and enjoy music.

Years after Peter Sellers had introduced me to marijuana, I told my brother-in-law at the time, Al, about a woman in Shepherd's Bush who he could buy cannabis from. Al is splendidly manic company, with a scattergun approach to humour and never afraid to make a bad joke, worth tolerating for the times when he hits the jackpot. One evening, I gave him a toke of a joint that really improved his strike rate, and he was very keen to know where I had got it. I told him that there was a lady in Shepherd's Bush who I called whenever I needed it but, just in case her telephone was being tapped, she liked her clients not to refer to grass when making orders, but to ask for a 'shirt', or more as required.

A couple of years later I got a message from Al asking for the number of my 'shirt maker'. I was quite surprised by this request because, while I consider myself reasonably well dressed, I don't think anyone had ever classified me as being in the sartorial stratosphere of, say, my father or Bryan Ferry. I obligingly sent the number back and thought no more about it. A few hours later Al rang me again saying I had given him the wrong number, so I gave it to him again, and shortly afterwards I got a rather agitated call from my shirt maker, Michael, saying he was being pestered by a lunatic, seemingly with my authority. Al, not well versed in the vernacular of scoring drugs, had insisted on repeating the line, 'I want some shirt' to the assumed dealer. While Michael was in the business of making and selling shirts, he did not expect orders to be placed using such an inexact quantitative unit, while Al laboured under the impression that maybe a coded discussion of his collar size might explain the details of his order. Happily, one telephone call from me to Michael clarified the situation and Al got his required delivery of shirt, and hopefully many hours of pleasure.

While I smoke cannabis from time to time, only very occasionally do I take ecstasy, which I tried for the first time in my fifties, during a trip to Ibiza. It gave me an overwhelming sense of affection towards everybody around me. I am not a particularly talented dancer, but it certainly encouraged me to feel the rhythm and believe, not only that I was dancing exceptionally well, but also that other people were looking at me and thinking the same thing, which of course in turn increases that feeling of love for everyone still further. It also opened up a whole genre of dance music that I wouldn't play of an evening at home, but that sounds absolutely fantastic as it vibrates through peaks and troughs on the dance floor.

The first time I went to Ibiza was at the invitation of Jemima Khan. Her marriage to Imran Khan had finally ended, so Jemima decided to celebrate by taking a house there and filling it with 'singles'. By then I was not strictly single, I was married with children, but sadly it was a description that applied to my life for much of the time. The trip didn't quite work out as I had envisaged, as Jemima arrived in the first flush of her affair with Hugh Grant, and they spent a great deal more time in bed than the rest of her guests, rarely venturing out to late-night functions. Luckily one of our group was the enigmatic Harry Stourton, who seemed to have an almost psychic knowledge of what was happening on the island, and the contacts to get us in to almost any party.

One night we arrived at a party and parked the car, and I bumped into a friend who offered me a puff of a joint. I duly accepted but then discovered that we were only in the car park, and we either had to wait for a bus or walk up to the top of a hill to actually get to the party itself. I was keen to set off quickly but after a while I realised that the joint had been considerably stronger than normal and this, combined with the serious exertion of climbing the hill, was making me feel a bit weird. I became paranoid that I might have a heart attack and die on this final hedonistic quest. Luckily, I was accompanied by the interior designer Rita Konig, who calmed me down and we eventually reached the top of the hill, albeit in my case soaked with sweat, a little worse for wear.

I was quite surprised to suddenly hear a voice calling me from across the room saying, 'My goodness me, I've been following you in *Tatler* for twenty years, and I think you're frightfully glamorous.' I looked up to see Patsy Tilbury walking towards me. This turned out to be something of a 'Doctor Livingstone I Presume' moment, and after a few minutes' conversation, I totally relaxed and melted into the whole atmosphere of music and party people, and really began to believe that in Ibiza I might have found my spiritual home. It was also the start of a friendship with the Tilbury family, who have a cast of characters you couldn't invent.

Lance and Patsy Tilbury were at the heart of London's swinging Sixties scene before moving to Ibiza. In those days the island was very basic and lacking in some amenities that you would take for granted nowadays, and they eked out a genuinely hippy existence. Lance, who sadly died in 2022, was an artist and loved the freedom of the life there and was able to indulge his hobby of smoking superhuman quantities of marijuana without ever getting totally wasted. Patsy too settled happily into this bohemian lifestyle, although, even now, her conversation exhibits a rather splendid contrast between their peace and love existence, on the one hand, and rogue incursions from the *Daily Mail* political handbook on the other.

She and Lance had two daughters, Charlotte and Leah. While her childhood was wonderfully unconventional, Charlotte has a natural business acumen and has become a tycoon in the beauty industry, building a cosmetic empire. She has never indulged in drugs of any kind, but there is a theory that, rather like Obelix in the *Asterix the Gaul* books, she must have fallen into a vat containing extreme stimulants as a baby, which gave her the astonishing energy of which she seems to have an inexhaustible supply: I have seen her gyrating on the dance floor in a wild manner that mere mortals would be unable to initiate without some form of input. On these occasions DJs shake in their boots when she decides that their music does not satisfy the levels of thrusting grind she wishes to express, and the situation tends to be remedied with some alacrity.

Charlotte and her husband George Waud have become close friends of mine. George is a film and theatre producer and is also involved in the racing world. I like to think that his relationship with Charlotte is akin to that of a racehorse trainer who sometimes needs to gently guide a remarkably gifted and spirited animal in the right direction. Charlotte and George are known for giving legendary parties, and we have been lucky enough to host one or two of these at Badminton.

*

Ibiza still features in my life and the person I am now feels a world away from the awkward nineteen-year-old who started a six-month internship at Sebag's stockbrokers. I had little grasp then of where the future would take me. The only near certainty was that I would one day inherit Badminton, so it made sense that I should embark on a degree in rural estate management at Cirencester Agricultural College. It was a requirement of the course that one did a year's practical, either on a farm or in a land agent's office, before starting, so I plumped for the easy option of electing to work for Humberts, who ran the estate office at Badminton.

This meant living at The Cottage and wandering down to the office every day. The resident land agent there, Tim Mitchell, was nearing retirement, and I loved sitting in his office listening to descriptions of the characters and machinations of estate life. He never seemed hurried by anything. On one occasion I remember him gazing out of the window for five minutes at workmen bricklaying on an adjoining building site. I was expecting some pearl of wisdom about estate maintenance, but he finally just turned to me and said rather sagely, 'There's tricks in every trade, Harry.'

Based in London for much of my training, I worked in the office of Humberts, which meant I spent most of the time going to expensive restaurants and casinos with other male friends. I was fascinated by gambling and delighted when Tim Hanbury said he had devised a failsafe system for winning at roulette. We spent many evenings carefully recording every spin of the wheel until the theoretical moment for a substantial bet had arrived. For a short time this was moderately successful but, to add to our problems, it was incredibly boring work, and we were unable to resist occasionally charging over to other tables between spins to alleviate this, which in itself defeated the object of what we were trying to do and tended to dwindle any earnings. We eventually reached the inevitable but painful conclusion that the system was not foolproof at all – no matter how assiduously we studied mathematical probability we were defeated by the fact that the wheel has no memory.

Although Cirencester lacked the intellectual rigour of a university, it was three years of studying something I was interested in. I was quite surprised how my time away from the academic world blunted the ease with which I could cram for exams, and I only just passed in the first year. It could perhaps also be said I didn't help myself by going to London every Wednesday and not returning until Friday morning, thereby missing a whole day of lectures.

There were quite a few students on the course who I knew to a greater or lesser extent from Eton, but the person I developed a lifelong friendship with was Jonathan Coltman-Rogers. Jonathan had been in the same house as me at Eton but was a couple of years younger, and my main memory of him was of a rather greedy boy already queueing for second helpings as cool characters like me scrambled into breakfast at the last minute. This proved fortunate for me because for some reason I had always liked the idea of having a friend I could nickname 'Fat Boy', and his love of food at least partially justified the name, despite the fact he wasn't actually fat. He remains universally known by this name to this day, and even his wife, Sophie, refers to him as 'Fatty'.

Fat Boy was phenomenally lazy. As someone with inclinations in this direction myself I couldn't help but be impressed by his ability to pass exams with minimal effort and to make himself busy by doing very little indeed. Fat Boy's father had died young, but his grandfather Guy was still alive and living at Stanage, the estate in Wales that he would inherit. Guy was very frail and, when I stayed there, we would go up and see him in his bedroom, where he informed me that three generations of his family had been on the bill (sent to the headmaster) at Eton for swearing, and he seemed particularly proud of his grandson for keeping up this tradition. I had heard parents expressing similar pride about their offspring being, say, the third generation of Masters of the Beagles, but a champion of bad language was a title less commonly aspired to. There was no doubt Fat Boy was something of a specialist in this field of endeavour, enjoying the various combinations of words that could constitute the ultimate in rudeness, but also the lazy camaraderie of saying 'hello' followed by a swear-word rather than a name. Never delivered with aggressive intent, this often astonished people meeting him for the first time.

In the summer break Fat Boy and I went on a camping holiday in Europe. Our main destination was St Tropez, often in the news as the ultimate location for the permissive lifestyle, embodied by spectacular actress Brigitte Bardot, who had a house there. When we arrived, however, it was very late in the day, and we couldn't find a campsite that wasn't full. Just when we thought we were going to have to sleep on the side of the road, we got lucky and gratefully pitched our tent.

Next morning, full of anticipation for what St Tropez had to offer, I poked my head out of the tent: before my gaze was everything I could possibly have hoped for. Naked people wandered about, and one couple in particular were showing more than just a friendly interest in each other. I shook a rather reluctant Fat Boy awake and insisted we leave the tent at once to avail ourselves of these pleasures; sure enough, on closer inspection *everyone* was naked, and we could only assume St Tropez was indeed the sexual paradise we had dreamt of and more. The reality, of course, was that we had stumbled into a nudist colony, and when the other participants saw these fully clothed Englishmen ogling them, they turned quite aggressive, and we were chased to our car with shouts of '*Allez-vous-en . . . voyeurs!*'

My friends and I raised eyebrows in London too. Regularly we would go to Annabel's, the nightclub started by Mark Birley in the 1960s, after dinner. Mark had impeccable taste and the club was ideal for some outrageous flirting, and one was always likely to bump into friends and acquaintances there. The waiters were very much of the old school and tolerant of degrees of behaviour after a few cocktails that might be unacceptable in the modern age. Even they, however, drew the line one night when I rediscovered my childhood pleasure of pretending that I was a horse, and, deciding that the cocktail tables were show jumps, began leaping over them with full sports commentary, before crashing to the floor and taking quite a few glasses of other less-than-happy clients with me. I was quite lucky not to suffer a lengthy ban.

I was not the only one who used Annabel's as a playground for the wilder extremes of silliness. One night Tim Hanbury arrived looking rather furtive and slightly shaken. It transpired he had been on a pub crawl with two friends, John Parry and Paddy Dodd-Noble. They had come across a double-decker bus full of Japanese tourists, left outside a pub with the engine ticking over while the driver went inside to relieve himself. This was too much to resist, and John leapt into the driver's seat with the rallying cry, 'Come on lads, Annabel's or bust.'

The other two climbed aboard and there followed a fearsome journey through the streets of London, damaging several cars on both sides of the road while the tourists on the upper floor screamed with terror. Eventually John crashed the bus completely, by which time there were police cars in pursuit with sirens blaring. John and Paddy ran for it, but Tim sauntered off as the police arrived, pointing vaguely in the direction of the fugitives with the words, 'I think they went that way officer.' He then hailed a cab and instructed it to go to Annabel's, while the other two were arrested and lucky not to be jailed in the trial that followed.

Around this time, I started playing poker with a group of friends; we made a bad initial mistake, incorporating a rule that we didn't have to pay up until the end of the year, a recipe for debts spiralling out of control. The person who came out worst was Johnny Hesketh, known to all his friends as The Captain, who owed nearly £2,000. This was the mid-1970s, so in today's money it corresponded to in excess of £15,000. We all reasoned therefore that, as it was at least theoretically a friendly game, a formula should be devised to reduce his debt.

The Captain was a man of substantial girth, with appetites to match. He was universally popular, but a lifestyle of excess suggested it was unlikely he would make old bones. One example of this was that he possessed the rare skill of being able to pour an entire bottle of sloe gin into his mouth as if he were a car being filled up with petrol. He was also a very heavy smoker.

It was decided that The Captain's debt could be reduced to £500 on condition that he gave up smoking for a month. He gratefully accepted this offer but, as the days went by, we continued to hear reports he was taking no notice of the smoking ban. Given the extent of our generosity, we decided he couldn't be allowed to get away with this and that it would be worth hiring a private detective to try to catch him *in flagrante delicto*.

We were due to play poker later that week in the Turf Club and, while he would not be able to smoke in front of us during the game, we were fairly certain he would light up the moment he left the building. The detective positioned himself opposite the front door of the club and waited, camera at the ready, but things did not go to plan. When The Captain finally appeared, he did not produce a cigarette but instead started to urinate in the street. He was blessed with a gift I have never seen before or since, producing an incredibly powerful jet stream, sometimes reaching more than twenty feet. On this occasion he displayed his ability to the full, right in front of the stunned detective, narrowly missing the car in which he was seated, and walked off into the night without lighting the tell-tale cigarette.

We were now quite seriously out of pocket but decided we should have one more try to catch him. We knew he was flying to Scotland the following weekend, so we bought the detective a ticket on the same plane and instructed him to place himself strategically directly behind The Captain. This was in the days when smoking was permitted on aeroplanes and, sure enough, the moment the seat-belt light pinged, he lay back in his seat and lit up. This was all described in a detailed report by the detective, in which he included 'exhibit A', the offending cigarette, and the observation that 'the subject seemed to enjoy the cigarette'. With this wealth of evidence against him, The Captain could not but pay up, although he had the last laugh, paying in £1 notes that he had cut in half.

Considering the distraction of my social life, I was slightly surprised that after three years at Cirencester I left with a degree, albeit a third class – not impressive but not surprising in view of the amount of work done. There was, however, still a practical exam to pass, which involved another two years working at Humberts, before I became a fully fledged chartered surveyor.

I definitely didn't want to drift into being a land agent, and my principal concern for the next year was to finish off the qualification. I started thinking about a proper career. Tim Hanbury was at a similar stage, having just passed his accountancy exams, so we made the decision that it would be a good idea to pool our talents and start a business together. This was not, in fact, a good idea as we were not exactly a dream team, the talent pooling being more suited to hedonistic activities. The projects we chose to research, namely rabbit farming and exporting agricultural machinery, were singularly unsuited to any of our abilities. Nonetheless, we formed a company called Herestar and spent a lot of time touring the country talking to experts in these fields, who must have been inwardly laughing at this pair of idiots, before wisely deciding not to invest any further time or money in such ideas.

There was some doubt as to whether I would pass the chartered surveyor practical exam as, what with all my gallivanting, I hadn't actually done much practical work. I attended a few refresher courses and was pleasantly surprised to pass, which meant that I could now add the initials ARICS after my name. I think it probably says more about the laziness and general attitudes of Etonians than my intelligence, but I was the only one of the fifteen or so who started the course five years earlier who actually achieved this objective, the others having either given up or failed the exams along the way.

The moment I finished the exams I gave up my job at Humberts and there followed a rather perfect summer, mainly with my friend Ben Collins, who eventually went on to set up a successful wine business. At this stage Ben had inherited enough money to ski all winter, drive a Porsche and generally enjoy the good things of life. He owned a Chelsea town house where we would meet up every day and plan activities. I became lifelong friends with Ben and his wife Angel until his tragic death in a car accident in 2021.

Unencumbered, Ben and I were able to devote ourselves fully to a life of leisure, going to parties, playing golf and tennis, attending Ascot and Test matches, and hanging out with people who seemed to have a similar amount of time on their hands. Staying at Ben's was a decadent Australian called Jimmy Armstrong who had originally been a friend of Ben's older brother, Chris. Chris had grown out of him, so Jimmy simply transferred his friendship to the younger of the two brothers. Jimmy was at least ten years older than us but a real Peter Pan figure, incapable of taking any relationship seriously. He was a major gambler and splashed his money around on girls and generally enjoying himself. That summer of hedonism he was the perfect compadre.

Ben and I continued the summer by taking the entourage of girls to his family house in the south of France. However, when we returned to an autumnal London the magic was somehow gone, and I realised that a life of total leisure was not the answer. In this respect my father came to the rescue and, via his great friend Jacob Rothschild, an interview for me was arranged with Michael Laurie and Partners, a small but dynamic firm of commercial property agents. This had the dual advantage of taking me into an environment where there was a good chance of making some money and using my chartered surveyor qualification to some purpose, as there was quite a lot of overlap between the urban and rural versions of the profession. The time had come to put away childish things . . . at least theoretically.

CHAPTER 5

The Marquess Bursts Forth

On my horse Irish Stew, in whom I had total trust
but limited control over.

THE PROSPECT OF the new job in London got my blood flowing because I could construct the fantasy that I might grow very rich from business. I had recently bought a one-bedroom flat in Bayswater, a good base from which to conduct operations, and it felt good to have joined that fabled world of work, in which previously I had only marginal involvement.

The leading light at Michael Laurie and Partners was Elliott Bernerd, who subsequently went on to make a serious fortune. I suspect one of the reasons he took me on was that he wanted to improve the image of respectability around the firm, and possibly felt that as I was an heir to a duke-dom, this impression would be enhanced. In my early days there I got lucky with a couple of deals and there may have been a vague perception that I was something of a natural at the game. The truth is that I was never really comfortable in the predatory world of business and, even then, I had suspicions that I would have been happier in a less cut-throat and more creative environment.

My supposed talent for the job was enhanced further when I was approached by Rupert Galliers-Pratt, who was seeking funding for a property he wanted to purchase. Rupert was universally known as The Chairman, possibly because he was unashamedly obsessed with money. From a young age he had worn the most enormous glasses, perhaps a useful device in concealing what he was thinking, but he was also incredibly funny and fascinated by some of the slightly dodgy characters of the property world. Over the years he has made and lost several fortunes but, when he has been up, his extravagance and generosity have been legendary, including large boats and villas in the south of France.

At the time, the property market lay in the doldrums, following the boom and bust of the early 1970s, and banks remained very cautious about lending. This left the door ajar for some good deals out there, if you could find the investors. Rupert was hoping my family money, along with my association with the rising star Elliott, might be the answer to this problem. I consulted my father and we duly bought the property, selling it on for a substantial profit soon afterwards. This had the dual benefit of getting my father quite excited about my money-making skills and increasing my reputation at Michael Laurie, although the truth of the matter was that my involvement was essentially limited to the initial introduction to Rupert.

Even this early, I sensed doubts about whether I was really in the right line of business. While I enjoyed the general banter about money with friends, I did not enjoy the act of salesmanship and trying to persuade people to buy something I didn't really believe in. I was also slightly unwilling to socialise with people from work, which limited my capability of using charm as a vehicle for business. Then there was the fact that, while I was delighted to be back in London, this did encourage certain aspects of hard living, and I was not always in prime condition for a long day in the office.

While I lived for the social aspect of London, I needed the country too – the fresh air and open space, and time to recharge ahead of another full week balancing work and parties. At the weekends I would retreat to Badminton and, inevitably, that meant hunting on Saturdays. In the 1980s when I was in my thirties, I was still hunting regularly. The enjoyment was almost entirely due to a wonderful horse I had called Irish Stew, over whom I had very little control but total trust; he would jump any fence I turned him to. As a result, I went as well as anyone in the field and the thrill of the slight terror at the thought of jumping a succession of hedges followed by the elation of having conquered that fear, offers as much pleasure as one can get from any sport.

The inevitable problem came when, after nearly fifteen years, this magnificent beast reached the end of his distinguished career, and I never found a similar connection with any replacement. I fairly quickly lost my nerve and gave up. Even now, members of the rather obsessive hunting community sometimes enquire rather heartily, 'When are we going to get you back on a horse, Harry?' to which the answer is a very firm, 'Never.' I loved those hunting days but certainly don't miss them now, although I have a strong belief in people's right to do it and its value in the rural community, as well as being proud to continue the family tradition of being a joint Master of the Beaufort Hunt.

In 1984, however, I was still very keen, which was lucky as it would have been a great disappointment to Master had I given up. Despite his advancing years he continued to hunt, albeit between increasing periods when for one reason or another he was not fit to do so. This perhaps created an illusion of immortality around him, and it was quite a surprise when he died a mere two months after his last foray on to the hunting field, becoming gravely ill when he was following the hunt in a Land Rover. He was bed-bound for only a few days before he died.

In the bubble that is Badminton, the death of Master was a major event. He had been the Duke living at Badminton for over sixty years and it was somehow hard for the local community to imagine anyone else in the role. My father was with him at the end, and then headed back to The Cottage, where he was very surprised to instantly receive a condolence telephone call from Sunny Marlborough, who was of course now his fellow Duke. Might there be some underground ducal communications network transmitting such information to the select few? He could think of no other way that Sunny could have heard about the death so quickly. This was followed a couple of hours later by a visit from the joint Master of the Hunt, Gerald Gundry, who wanted to give some gentle advice to my father about his new role. I watched as he sat lugubriously on the club fender repeating, 'Saddest day I've ever known, saddest day I've ever known.'

The condolences flooded in, and the newspapers, even across the pond, paid tribute to Master. The *New York Times* described him as 'Renowned as a Fox-hunter,' and almost every obituary headline included the word 'hunting'.

On the day of the funeral, my brother Johnson, who was eighteen at the time and who has always had a surreal mind, enquired as to whether we should expect helicopters hovering above the church to get the best television pictures, but it turned out to be, of course, just a very well-attended but traditional affair. The Queen came with most of the senior Royals, including the Queen Mother and the Prince and Princess of Wales. The short service included 'All Things Bright and Beautiful', which our land agent insisted was Master's very favourite hymn – none of us had attended church often enough to disabuse him of this notion. Master had gone to church every Sunday, but possibly this was nothing to do with his being particularly religious, more that he was a man who liked routine, a characteristic that had perhaps also made him continue hunting long after he had really enjoyed it.

When the service ended, the family went out to the grave to watch the burial. Mary stood a few steps in front of everyone while a trumpeter played as Master was laid to rest. After a few moments, the Queen and Queen Mother went forward to comfort her. Mary, who had become a frail figure in her old age, took the arm of my father and I was surprised to see him sobbing uncontrollably. Although he was very different from Master, a strong mutual fondness and respect had grown between them over the years. But he was also perhaps feeling an awareness of the responsibility that now fell on his shoulders.

My father slotted into the role of duke fairly seamlessly. The gamekeeper and a couple of other senior employees had come round for a Christmas drink the year before Master died and, after a few whiskies, had remarked about how difficult it would be to fill Master's shoes. He replied with an air of nonchalant wisdom that it would be a mistake to try to copy completely the ways of his predecessor. This became evident when Master's chauffeur came up just after his death and said rather kindly that he was there to do anything he could to help, to which my father replied, in a fit of perhaps debatably mock anger, 'Of course there is. You work for me now.'

Over the years my mother had been unambiguous about wanting to move into Badminton, but my father expressed doubts, although he probably always intended to do so, if remotely possible. Master had not been an extravagant man, but he had subsidised the hunt to a huge degree, and even living fairly modestly in a house of Badminton's size is very expensive. This meant that, despite some sensible tax planning keeping death duties to a reasonable level, my father also inherited substantial borrowings that had to be serviced, alongside the running costs of the house.

Two things made it possible for my parents to take on this daunting task. The first was that the Marlborough Gallery had gone from strength to strength, which meant my father was able to pay quite a lot of the running expenses out of his personal money. The second was that in the ballroom quietly lurked the monumental Badminton Cabinet, commissioned in Florence by the 3rd Duke in 1726, and which had taken thirty-six years to make. My father sold it for in excess of £8 million, at the time the highest price ever paid for a piece of furniture. This paid off most of the debt, although there was something of an outcry when the cabinet was inevitably bought by an American and was set to leave the country. When confronted by the press about this my father rather languidly commented, 'It was only a cupboard of which I was not particularly fond.' Rather irritatingly, it was sold on about twenty years later for £19 million, the heiress who had bought it from us complaining it was too big for her home.

There is another empty space in the North Hall where the huge third-century Badminton Sarcophagus, which depicts

The Triumph of Dionysos and the Seasons, used to stand until 1955 when some Americans came to lunch at Badminton with Master and Mary and requested a tour of the house. They seemed particularly interested in the Sarcophagus, which had been purchased by the third Duke on his European tour, and casually asked Master at what price he might consider selling it. Master's knowledge of art was limited and after a few moments' thought he suggested £5,000 as the largest figure he could imagine, and he was quite surprised how quickly he was able to seal the deal.

He did briefly mention this to my father, but at this time there was still an element of uncertainty about my father's position as the heir apparent, and as Master was so delighted with the sale and needed the money in the years of 98 per cent top-rate taxation, he thought that it might be inappropriate to counsel against it. It was not an area of the art market in which my father had any speciality, and while he suspected there might be an element of underselling, he was as surprised as anyone about what subsequently happened. A short time afterwards the American press was full of self-congratulatory stories of how the Met Museum in New York had acquired this 'priceless' piece.

A few years later my mother was in New York and went to the Metropolitan Museum, where she came across the Sarcophagus. It was in a very prominent place, roped in with a permanent security guard on hand. Somehow this invoked in her a feeling of what might have been, and she started trying to climb over the ropes crying out, 'That really belongs to me,' before being led away by guards, well trained in handling occasional visits from troublesome lunatics. I don't know what the valuation would now be, but it would surely dwarf that of the Badminton Cabinet that my father sold for such a substantial sum on his accession.

With other relics remaining, and paintings known to be at the house, Badminton requires a sophisticated alarm system, but the original one installed by my parents tended to go off for no reason quite often. My mother was frequently alone in the house, and when this happened, she would go downstairs, taking with her as a precaution her faithful spaniel Toby, and go through the laborious process of resetting it. Therefore, when the alarm went off yet again, she was not particularly frightened and trudged downstairs to deal with it. She entered the library and, as she opened the door, saw a man with a swag bag across his shoulder selecting further pieces to put into it. She was obviously shocked but Toby, who had some previous with regard to savagery and had bitten the local vicar so badly he needed stitches, went for the man full throttle, causing him to drop the bag and flee in terror of his life. The police were called, and the papers were full of the story of the 'have a go' Duchess, but she was determined that the real hero was Toby, and he was pictured in all the stories.

My parents embarked on a major refurbishment of Badminton. The most important part was a complete renewal of the boiler and central heating. Master had been oblivious to cold; my father said that when he had stayed there before moving to The Cottage it was colder than anything he had experienced in the army, and sometimes he had to wear an overcoat in bed. Their real achievement, however, was to transform what had previously been a rather impersonal house into a well-decorated family home, with much more of a lived-in feel.

They also undertook a major improvement of the garden, putting in new flowerbeds and other features. I think it was occasionally a subject of discord between my parents, as my father was prone to doing things without consultation. Once they had quite a row, with my mother complaining, 'Box, box, box, box. All it is, is box.' The reality, however, was that their combined skills did create something special.

Master's widow Mary stayed on in the house, becoming a rather ghostly figure. In her late eighties, she wandered around increasingly unaware of her surroundings and spent most of her time watching television so loudly in her upstairs room that it could be heard all the way through parts of the house. She died three years later, joining Master in the family burial garden.

When my father had just become Duke the whole family faced another adjustment: as we were not direct descendants of Master, on his death, from one day to the next, we all changed from being plain mister or miss to having various titles. My father obviously became Duke of Beaufort, which

was a high-profile enough change for everyone to be aware
who he now was. I, though, became the Marquess of
Worcester. It was particularly difficult at work to ring clients
and say it was Harry Worcester, having previously been
Harry Somerset. They naturally had no idea who I was without my going through a tortured explanation, a procedure I
found very awkward. I still find my title a little embarrassing, and there's a part of me that feels that any respect it
garners is not totally deserved.

In typical style Johnson turned this into an imaginary
soap opera, providing a running commentary on the activities of these new various characters: His Grace, The
Marquess, Lord Edward etc. For example, when I helped
myself to a whisky from the drinks tray, he would announce,
'Of course the Marquess loves his whisky.' He built some
very amusing narratives around this but, unfortunately,
when a rather grand dowager came to lunch, he did not
explain that the whole thing was a *joke*, and my father heard
a few days later that she was complaining to her friends
about how families who inherited their titles through the
back door tended to get ridiculously over-excited by their
elevation.

As Master of the Horse, Master took part in royal occasions where horses and carriages were involved. This
included the wedding of the Queen to Prince Philip in 1947
and the 1953 Coronation. Most years he stayed with the
Queen at Windsor Castle for Royal Ascot. In their younger

days the Royal Family used to ride around the course at
Ascot in the morning and Master was often alongside the
Queen.

After Master's death, as a token of respect, my parents
were asked in 1984 to stay at Windsor for Ascot but, much
to my mother's annoyance, my father politely declined the
invitation on the grounds that he didn't like racing. It was
therefore rather a pleasant surprise when I received a call
from an equerry asking me to deputise.

I was issued with detailed instructions about exactly what
time I should arrive, but disaster struck when my car
suddenly broke down on the elevated section of the Windsor
bypass, about a mile away from the castle. It was a boiling
hot day, and I was wearing a top hat and tails, so to have any
chance of arriving on time there was no choice but to leave
my car behind and run, desperately trying to hitch a lift at
the same time. I was pouring with sweat and probably did
not present the perfect image of someone motorists would
feel inclined to help out, but finally a good Samaritan did
stop and was most surprised when I asked him to take me
to the private entrance to Windsor Castle.

I arrived looking extremely dishevelled, but the smooth
machinery of the royal entourage took over, first of all
suggesting discreetly that I might like to clean up before
heading off to the races, and then arranging for my car to be
picked up.

I didn't quite know what to expect staying at Windsor,

but my main fear was that all conversation would be very stilted and formal. This turned out not to be the case and there was quite a lot of laughter. I couldn't help but be impressed by the organisation of the whole thing, with everyone being told such details as which carriage they would be travelling to the races in well in advance. Once we got to the races we were allowed to go down from the royal box and mix with friends below, which provided an outlet to let one's hair down further.

Most members of the Royal Family were there and seating plans at dinner were organised around a strict rota based on precedence, so it was possible to work out who you would be seated by at the next meal. I eventually sat on the Queen's left, and conversation flowed easily enough although, as the monarchy is meant to have no political views, there was a vague limitation on subject matter. Perhaps the most touching moment was when the Queen took the party out on to the battlements after dinner, from where we could observe human life going about its business below on the streets of Windsor unaware of our watching them. She seemed quite excited about this covert viewing. There was something decidedly girlish about her enthusiasm, allowing a charming and unexpected glimpse of her character that I had not been privy to before or since.

CHAPTER 6

Tatler's Number-One Eligible Bachelor

With Imran Khan and Liza Campbell at Annabel's.

IN 1985 *TATLER* picked me as their number-one most eligible bachelor. At the time I was living in Chelsea with a friend, Laura Elliot, as a lodger. Laura often came down to Badminton with me for the weekend, something that delighted my father as she was very obliging in telling him about everything I had been up to – he named her his 'Spy in the House of Love'. There was no doubt I was providing plenty of material for her espionage. I was having to juggle a number of girls around, even on occasion having to return home during my lunch hour to fulfil my duties. I can't totally explain this sudden success with women, but I suppose since Master's death I had a higher profile and was just generally developing in confidence and self-belief. I cannot deny I was quite pleased with this profile. *Tatler* spoke of me as being 'disarmingly vulnerable' and of girls 'champing at the bit' to date me, albeit with the caveat that I was one of the 'clumsiest men in Europe'. The profile also described an incident, apocryphal, of my dropping a lit cigarette into a log basket and then kneeling down and trying to remedy this by throwing a load of logs over my shoulders in an attempt to retrieve it. A similar incident, however, did actually take place where some guacamole from a canapé was somehow diverted from its passage towards my mouth and ended up in a rather grand lady's Gucci handbag. She was both bewildered and displeased – in that order – to find me throwing its contents all over the room in a desperate, probably unsuccessful, attempt to minimise staining.

My great level of desirability was slightly unexpected. I was a late developer, perhaps not helped by the fact that I didn't need to shave until after I had left Eton. Mildly embarrassing, it was also an excuse to continue behaving like a child, which included a total inability to communicate with girls. As a teenager, parties were a nightmare of awkwardness as I dragged some unfortunate girl on to the dance floor, and then lumbered around doing something resembling a waltz while making extremely stilted conversation. This might have gone on forever had I not met the Mancroft girls, who lived in a nearby village. The eldest, Victoria, was about my age but considerably more sophisticated. My initial suspicion was that she was out of my league, but the good news was that, unlike other girls, she did share the same sense of humour as me, as well as an enjoyment of petty rebellions such as smoking. Both she and her sister

Jessica quickly became regulars at The Cottage and have remained friends ever since.

The total absence of girls at Eton had fostered a general culture of interest in other boys, and during school I often heard phrases like 'stop tarting', addressed to some of the prettier boys. My participation in any form of actual homosexuality was relatively limited, but my great friend Kershaw and I did make a list of the ten best-looking boys in the school. We then gave each of the boys a number and created a game, basically a variation of Snap, whereby the first of us who saw the boy in question would shout out his number and score a point. Simple enough when walking to chapel in the morning, but sometimes it grew more competitive, and we would go into the boy's house and race as fast as we could round the passages in order to be the first to record a sighting. This also introduced an element of danger into the game, and I remember Kershaw falling down an entire flight of stairs in his desperate quest for points. For the sake of variation, we included a red-faced and rather fat boy, who was certainly no beauty but scored a point under the codename 'Elevenos'.

When I left school, I was still rather uncomfortable with girls at formal parties. The debutante scene was on its last legs in an official sense. Girls were no longer being presented to the Queen as they had been a few years earlier, but a vague adherence to some of the rituals gave an excellent excuse to give a party. In the summer of 1970, the coming-out party of Catherine Guinness was expected to be the event of the season, but thinking I wouldn't know anyone there, I was not keen to attend. Eventually I was persuaded by my mother, who, despite the recent election of the Heath Conservative government, convinced herself that the occasion might be the last of its kind and that I should go as a witness to a dying ritual.

The ball, held at Catherine's mother's house, Kelvedon Hall in Essex, was indeed a rather splendid affair with everything done to the highest of standards, including a live band playing loud rock music. There were lots of girls and, while I failed to draw the most attractive ones into my orbit, I could see the potential that an endless round of parties could have for my social and sexual life. Unfortunately, on this occasion I failed to monitor the quantities of champagne consumed and was violently sick in the flowerbeds.

Something clicked at those summer parties, and I ended up kissing multiple girls. The turnaround in my romantic fortunes created a slightly unjustified belief that I was becoming some kind of stud, although despite some exploratory fumbling I was still a virgin. I had often heard friends discussing a legendary prostitute in the West End of London called Denise Bunny, who seemed to specialise in these matters, and I had even gone as far as looking her up in the telephone book.

I think it is fortunate that I never went down this route, as I later heard she was already very much of a certain age. I could have been put off for life. It wasn't until a camping trip around Europe with Kershaw that I finally got the monkey off my back. On a ferry to Greece, we saw two American girls getting on and noticed that one was really quite pretty, the other considerably less so. We bought some duty-free whisky in the hope this might encourage them to see the light and end up with one of us.

The plan was only partially successful in that the person who got most drunk was me. The party dispersed and I found myself sitting alone with one of the girls, whose opening question was whether I would like to come down to her cabin, a request I of course could not refuse. We got on very well indeed and I emerged triumphant, although the principal merit of my performance was speed of delivery.

Kershaw had already lost his virginity two days earlier, although in rather embarrassing circumstances. When we had been in Rome, with our friend Harry Fane, we had stayed with a family friend of Harry's parents, Fulke Warwick. Fulke, the 7th Earl of Warwick, had decided to exile himself there, in an enormous villa, Lord Marchmain-style, with his third wife and her stepdaughter. Given his age and background, we were not expecting to particularly enjoy our stay there, but we absolutely adored it and sat around with Fulke into the small hours listening to him being very funny and running through his reminiscences. It turned out that a lot of what he told us was pure fantasy: 'My dear boy, I like to think that I played my part in winning the war. Winston rang me up most days for my advice.' We fell for this hook, line and sinker and felt we were in the presence of greatness, although the reality was he had spent much of the war in Hollywood pursuing an acting career.

Fulke's stepdaughter had a German nanny who took rather a shine to Kershaw, and after a couple of days his prospects with her were looking good. They arranged a late-night liaison in the garden but underestimated the level of security that Fulke employed, and they were unlucky enough to trigger the alarm, causing the whole garden to light up and sirens to start wailing, and then be surrounded by a guard and three snarling Alsatians, while still *in flagrante delicto*.

Back on English soil, the season, and the main staple for meeting girls, was kicked off by Peter Townend, an incredibly snobbish man who had just retired as editor of *Burke's Peerage*. Every year in the spring he gave a drinks party for debutantes in his Chelsea flat, beneficial for him as it kept some version of the former glories of the London season alive, and obliged aspiring mothers to return the invitation when they gave a party for their daughters. For the 'eligible' crop of young men he invited, however, it was a wonderful opportunity to inspect all the girls who had recently arrived in London and, on the back of this, I was suddenly in great demand and embarked on a summer of what seemed like unparalleled success.

I felt there was room for improvement and couldn't help noticing that Robin Smith-Ryland was the most successful of my contemporaries with girls. I studied Robin closely and saw he had a way of using his rather large eyes to stare almost hypnotically at them, somewhat in the manner of the snake in the *Jungle Book* film, and they seemed to fall at his feet every time. I wasted a considerable amount of time staring at the mirror and contorting my face into what I thought was his failsafe seduction technique, but when I actually embarked on this approach, I was forced to reject it after several girls looked slightly alarmed and asked if I was feeling unwell.

Despite finally gaining in confidence, I still did not have a full-time girlfriend. This was remedied when I met a girl named Vanessa Kirk, and we were together for two or three years. We enjoyed some great times, but it perhaps wasn't the ideal arrangement for her as, apart from holidays, we met only about once a week. These meetings often constituted dinner with other couples, with the men tending to dominate proceedings with braying conversation.

I then went out with another girl, Louisa D'Abo, who had to endure a similar regime of occasional meetings. Once again, I was very fond of her but couldn't see it going any further, so I ended it, perhaps a trifle insensitively. A couple of days later I was quite surprised to receive a call from Louisa's brother, Henry, summoning me round to his house.

Their father had recently died and, although he was only in his early twenties, Henry felt it his duty to take on a sort of *pater familias* role. It was therefore a bit like going to the headmaster's study and being told in Henry's deep, slightly gurgling voice, 'You've behaved very badly, and I want to talk to you about it.'

Henry then gave me a whisky and I explained that, while I had every intention of my break-up with Louisa being on the friendliest of terms, sometimes relationships don't work out for the long term. He grunted but seemed to accept the gist of my explanation and we had another whisky, then another and another . . . until finally we were talking together like old friends. We remain great friends to this day.

One of the pleasures of seeing Henry is to activate his laugh, which goes off like a crow scarer, but in a deeply resonant tone. I have always found it infectious. This view was seemingly shared by Mary Beaufort in the latter days of her life, when she was sitting at a dinner at The Cottage in total silence, as was her sad fate by then. Henry was there and unleashed the laugh on the heels of some remark by my father; the sudden cacophony seemed to stimulate some long-forgotten sensation from deep within, and Mary emerged briefly into the world and joined in the hysterics.

I had another girlfriend, Lucinda Trehearne, a wonderfully independent Gloucestershire girl happy that our meetings tended to be relatively occasional but all the more powerful for that when they happened. This enabled us both to live other lives, and suddenly I found myself going out with quite a succession of girls, sometimes overlapping.

A more unexpected but thrilling tryst was with Jerry Hall.

I met her through Rupert and Josephine Loewenstein, who were great friends of my parents. Rupert became the financial manager of the Rolling Stones, He had made a considerable amount of money as a merchant banker by the time he met Mick Jagger in the late Sixties. The Rolling Stones were at this stage one of the biggest bands in the world but, like many of their contemporaries, found themselves tied into unsatisfactory contracts and made nothing like as much money as they should have done. Rupert could not be described as a leading figure in the counterculture, but neither was he a typical banker, and he persuaded Mick that his financial affairs would be best managed by his bank. They both started to make a lot of money from this arrangement. Eventually things were going so well that Rupert decided to leave the bank and devote himself full time to the Stones.

I think Mick appreciated not only his financial genius but also his wonderful sense of humour, which included a unique way of raising his eyes skyward when describing some mildly unfortunate event. I asked Rupert about the latest state of play on Keith Richard's heroin addiction, very relevant in a business sense as Keith's drug convictions were threatening the possibility of his getting a visa for the forthcoming American tour. Rupert looked at me and replied in a matter-of-fact voice, 'Well he's absolutely fine now . . . but next time the washing machine breaks down, who knows?', followed by the inevitable upward movement of his eyes and a resigned sigh. The family friendship continues to this day and Rupert's daughter, Dora, who has inherited her father's wit, is a great friend and lives in the village at Badminton.

In 1981 Rupert and Josephine threw a ball for the twenty-first birthday of their son Konrad at their house in Gloucestershire. It was a lavish affair, and the theme stipulated that all women wore green, although Princess Margaret defiantly wore a bright pink ball dress. Mick was another guest of honour and, when I sat down at my table for dinner, I was rather excited to find myself placed next to Jerry Hall.

Jerry and I got on very well. She was not only beautiful but also used her sense of humour as a way of being flirtatious, and her southern drawl enhanced this further. I had now reached a stage where I quite fancied my skills as a womaniser, but my target audience tended to be based around the Sloane Square area, and to be getting on so well with such a star was more than I was accustomed to. Nonetheless, I didn't expect any more to come of it and simply left the party having much enjoyed meeting her.

It was therefore a pleasant surprise when, about six months later, I got a call from Jerry saying she was passing through London on her way back to America, and would I like to meet up for dinner. I of course accepted, and it was even more exciting when I discovered she was going through one of her periodic break-ups with Mick. Once again, we got on incredibly well and ended up going back to her hotel for a drink, and a few hours later I walked home beaming with pride.

I was not, at this stage in my life, full-blooded gossip column fodder, but Jerry obviously was, and I knew it was important to be totally discreet about the evening. For two days I managed to restrain myself, but eventually couldn't resist telling a couple of friends in strictest confidence. They were naturally impressed, and it wasn't that many days later that the floodgates opened, and everyone knew the story. There followed a small piece in the *Evening Standard* hinting at a friendship. By this time Jerry was back in America but I think she must have got wind of my boasting as, when somebody asked Jerry about me, she is reputed to have replied in her famous twang, 'If that boy's cock was as big as his mouth, he'd be one hell of a lay.'

Mick and Jerry later became friends of mine. I have stayed at their chateau in France, and they have both been to Badminton. Mick is something of a phenomenon. I have seen more Rolling Stones concerts than those of any other band, and every time it is hard not to think that it must be their last, but Mick has the energy of someone half his age. As they have such longevity, one tends to compare the Stones' continued displays of youthful vigour with growing older oneself, and when they once again triumph one almost feels their defying of gravity is a positive reflection of one's own ageing process. They are helped by their pedigree in the blues and their excellent musicianship, but Mick himself should never be underestimated in other spheres. He is more cultured and intelligent than most of his contemporaries, which may have made it easier to come to terms with the pressures of being the ultimate rock icon for over fifty years while others went off the rails.

The same year *Tatler* named me their most eligible bachelor, the number of my girlfriends slimmed down, and I found myself spending more and more time with Tracy Ward. Tracy, the beautiful sister of the actress Rachel Ward, who was now hot property in Hollywood, was just starting out on her own acting career. Tracy was a wonderful free spirit, with a slightly alternative way of looking at things, and had a wider range of friends than I did. I really liked the avenues this opened up, but also appreciated the way she didn't try to change my ways, and I felt generally relaxed with her. Coincidentally, she was also a great friend of Cosima Fry, who started going out with my brother Johnson, and we all spent quite a lot of time together.

Later that summer Tracy and I went on holiday in Italy and ended up staying at Cetinale, the beautiful Roman Baroque Tuscan villa where her mother, Claire Ward, lived with Tony Lambton. After our trip to Italy, Tracy went straight into shooting the second season of *C.A.T.S. Eyes* and I went back to my job. She was able to come to Badminton, or wherever else we were going for the weekend, and we generally had a very good time together, such that I began to think marriage might be on the cards.

C.A.T.S. Eyes was very popular in Australia and the producers of the show decided to fly Tracy out there after Christmas for a promotional tour. My brother Eddie's friend, Peter Jansen, had long been trying to persuade me to visit as well, so I decided to join Tracy once she had completed the work element of the trip. Our first stop was to stay with Tracy's sister Rachel and her husband, the Australian actor Bryan Brown. Rachel was perceived as being the most beautiful girl of her generation, but she was also something of a rebel and had found the limitations of upper-class London life a bit stifling. She therefore headed for America, where she had great success as a model, before her breakthrough film opposite Burt Reynolds, *Sharky's Machine*. The part she is probably best remembered for, however, is that of Meggie Cleary in the television series *The Thorn Birds*, where she also met Bryan.

Bryan was from a working-class background but gradually worked his way up the ranks of the film world, co-starring in films such as *Cocktail* with Tom Cruise, and *Gorillas in the Mist* with Sigourney Weaver. When Rachel and Bryan got engaged, Tracy and Rachel's mother Claire said she was very nervous about the first meeting with her rather unlikely son-in-law; by way of making conversation she said to him, 'Do you know, Bryan, I was only nineteen when I had Rachel,' to which Bryan replied in his Australian accent, 'Oh really, I was thirty-five.'

Tracy and I continued our tour with a trip to an island on

the Great Barrier Reef and I half had in mind this might be a good spot to propose marriage, but the place turned out to be more like a Butlin's holiday camp than a romantic hideaway, further damaged by an all-embracing smell of bird shit. We were trapped for three days, but the fact that Tracy managed to laugh about it made me more convinced of her suitability.

Returning to the mainland, we met up with my childhood friend Jed, who had emigrated to Australia when he left school, and also stayed with Peter Jansen in the rambling multi-storey warehouse he turned into his home. Tracy and I continued to get on well, but in fact my actual proposal came after a minor row we had about travel plans, and perhaps lacked the bended-knee romance that other couples indulge in.

When we got back to England, we decided to marry in June, which meant we had to prepare the whole thing in about four months. The plan was to get married after lunch, followed by a reception, and then for guests to leave and the select ones to return for a dance in the evening. Like many couples we became rather self-important about the whole thing and devised complicated categories of which people were included in the various different parts of the day.

One weekend during this period, a friend, Philip Dunne, was staying at Badminton and said that his friend Princess Diana was all alone at Highgrove, the country residence of Prince Charles, and would like to come to lunch. This was obviously very exciting for all members of the family, and in our different ways we were much taken with Diana's charisma. She was certainly not an intellectual but had a wonderful mode of conversation that was simultaneously slightly shy and almost, but not quite, flirtatious, as well as possessing a rather irresistible but restrained laugh.

Badminton was not open to the public, but parties could arrange visits by appointment. My mother was knowledge-able about the history of the house and used to conduct these tours. She was also very good at combining serious information with anecdotes about our ancestors. She was therefore delighted when after lunch Diana requested a quick tour, and the rest of us followed behind as my mother demonstrated her skills.

All went well until we reached the ballroom, which Eddie had been using to record some of his musical compositions on to cassettes, and then putting some artwork and silly titles on the plastic containers. As I walked in, I noticed one of these sitting on top of the grand piano and was concerned to see the title he had chosen for his masterpiece: 'Cunts I Have Known'.

I thought it would be prudent to remove this as quickly as possible, but my mother was now in full cry with her tour, and when she saw I was hiding something, she thought I might be depriving her audience of her words of wisdom on a key artefact. She defied my gentle protests, extracted it from my hand and showed it to everyone. Of course, she quickly realised it was inappropriate, but it was too late now, so she launched into a rather desperate piece of damage limitation and started telling a story about some friend of her father's. I can't remember exactly the lead-up, but I could not but be aware of the punchline, bellowed at the top of her voice, '. . . and she had a cunt like a carthorse!'

Everyone in the room was a bit stunned by this sudden turn of events, but to her credit the first person to start laughing was Diana, who seemed to have thoroughly enjoyed this display of eccentricity. I really felt she had been able to let her hair down with us, and a couple of days later I was telling my friend Dave Ker about it, while saying that I didn't feel I knew her well enough to ask her to our wedding. Dave looked absolutely horrified at this sacrilege, and shouted like an angry schoolmaster, 'Get that invitation out this instant, Harry!' I took the plunge and was rather delighted when she and Prince Charles accepted.

As the wedding drew nearer a number of my friends contacted me saying the tabloid press were trying to dig some dirt on me, ahead of what was being billed 'the wedding of the year'. I had not led a blameless life, but I don't think there were any real skeletons in the cupboard. Nonetheless, for the last couple of weeks before the marriage I was cautious, and the huge paparazzi contingent outside the stag party that Taki organised at Aspinalls were disappointed to find me leaving the casino poorer, but otherwise not too much the worse for wear.

The press did, however, manage to trick a former girl-friend into giving an interview about me and this ended up on the front page of the *News of the World* under the head-line 'C.A.T.S. Eyes girl stole my £100 million man'. It was reasonably complimentary about me, depicting me as a hard drinkin' good lovin' type, but there was one piece of complete rubbish in it, saying that my principal seduction technique was to lure girls into the conservatory at Badminton, and once in that environment they found me totally irresistible. The tabloid press was at its worst at this time, and whenever a politician was caught indulging in sexual shenanigans, it could almost invariably be relied upon to add the totally false allegation that he insisted on dressing in the shirt of the football team he supported before entering the bedroom, so I suppose this mythologising was par for the course.

The night before the wedding I stayed with Ben Collins and his wife Angel, who lived near Tracy's childhood home, Cornwell, where the wedding was set to take place, along with Johnson, who was my best man, and a number of other close friends. I gave lunch to the ushers at a local pub and then we set off for the church, where I was surprised by the number of people lining the road hoping for a glimpse of celebrities. After the service we had a traditional reception in the marquee at Cornwell and then rested prior to the party in the evening.

The guests were invited for 10.30pm and the music started at once. There was a heaving dance floor and a generally superb atmosphere. What was reported in the papers, however, was the behaviour of our highest-profile guests: Prince Charles and Princess Diana. It was at about this time that rumours of problems in the royal marriage were beginning to surface, and stories of Diana dancing maniacally with a succession of young men while Charles sat in a corner in close conversation with a former girlfriend added grist to the mill.

Tracy and I danced until dawn and went to bed satisfied that we had given a great party, and then set off the next day on our honeymoon. Tracy had set her sights on India, but in June it would have been stiflingly hot, so we diverted to Paris, starting with a night at the Ritz, and then over a period of a few days drove through Italy, down to Cetinale, where we were joined by a number of friends. I planned the journey around some three-star Michelin restaurants, but after the third night Tracy insisted on an alteration to the schedule as my excessive greed was having a negative effect on more traditional honeymoon duties. The whole trip was most enjoyable, and we returned to England much looking forward to our new life together.

Most weekends, Tracy and I would stay with my parents, who had fully adjusted to life at Badminton. They were hospitable about mixing our friends in with theirs and this provided for varied entertainment; often Monster was there too, creating some very entertaining late-night discussions with my mother. Neither of them was averse to the occasional drink, but this tended to fuel their intellect, with my mother in particular prone to walking around gesticulating during these sessions. Someone once commented that the room was like Spaghetti Junction when they were in full cry. Monster was in the process of writing her third book, a biography of Queen Elizabeth I, and her expertise at gleaning information from newspapers always meant she was incredibly well informed. Late at night, however, she was inclined to veer off on tangents, sometimes even more interesting than the original point.

At the time Monster was going out with Matthew Carr, a talented artist who had been discovered by Andy Warhol after Matthew had persuaded his parents to allow Warhol to use their house in Oxford to hold a party. On seeing Matthew's drawings, Warhol immediately put him up in the Ritz before taking him to America, where he launched his career. By the time Monster met him, Matthew was well established in the art world, but he was also a bit of a maverick, and there was always an element of unpredictability about him. This, though, provided the perfect foil to Monster's obliging nature, and she delighted in gently scolding him like he was a much-loved but badly behaved dog when he returned to his kennel. There was no doubt they adored each other.

They married in 1989 and Matthew's best man was Teddy St Aubyn, who was just embarking on a writing career. Most famous are his five Patrick Melrose novels, the last of which,

Mother's Milk, would gain a Booker prize nomination in 2006 and become a successful television series. These books were semi-autobiographical, including some harrowing scenes of child abuse and drug addiction, but also show off his biting wit and ability to pick up on barbed dialogue, and he was quite unembarrassed to aim his vicious pen at himself.

Matthew and Monster's wedding was attended by many beauties, including Jerry Hall. This provoked Dave Ker to liken my father, who normally disliked ceremonial duties, to a 'dog in a dustbin'. When Matthew died in 2011, aged only fifty-eight, Monster was devastated; she remarked recently that a day never passes without her thinking about him.

My brother Eddie had married Caroline, known as Carol, Davidson at Badminton a few years earlier. The vicar at the time was quite a character and, perhaps motivated by the inevitable drinks that would be offered, insisted on visiting my mother time and time again to discuss the order of service. This tested my mother's tolerance, and by the time he turned up for the fifth time she had rather given up listening. When he asked Carol if she was going to incorporate 'obey' into her wedding vows, my mother misheard and thought he had posed an inappropriate question about whether she was a virgin. She therefore admonished him furiously with the words, 'Vicar, this is too much!' and stormed from the room. Baffled, he left with his tail between his legs, which did at least have the effect of his daily visits ceasing, even after the misunderstanding had been cleared up. Johnson also married a couple of years later, having lived in America for two years with his girlfriend, Cosima Fry, but opted for a simpler registry office ceremony.

During the week, Tracy and I lived in London. I formed a property-dealing company as a joint venture with the partners of Morgan Grenfell Laurie. For the first two years this progressed well, but then one particular purchase went disastrously wrong: we bought a shop in an area that suddenly turned into a retail desert when Marks & Spencer shut down their nearby branch, and from that moment the whole thing turned into a salvage operation to minimise losses. Fortunately, the group who I worked with at MGL decided to break away and form their own agency, and they asked me to join them. I was paid a minimal salary but with very generous commission arrangements, which gave me the opportunity to make a lot of money without any of the overhead pressures normally associated with running a business. To start with I found myself working really hard with an element of success. The only trouble was that, when the market slumped, deals dried up and this had a bad effect on my always-fragile work ethic.

CHAPTER 7

Rock

Preparing to burst into song on stage with The Business Connection.

ONE OF MY main passions has always been music, and it was listening to the radio at prep school that first introduced me to the joy of it all. Even now, in my early seventies, I listen constantly in the car, and sunbathing, which I always loathed as a child, has been revolutionised by advances in suncream and top-quality headphones. I had high-end speakers installed in the library at Badminton the moment we moved in, where an evening's entertainment is always accompanied by some of the five thousand carefully selected tracks on my iPod. I can also still remember the moment when I decided to give up my job in commercial property, driving across Europe while blasting out Led Zeppelin's 'Kashmir' and Hendrix's 'Purple Haze'.

Being able to listen to my favourite music whenever I like still feels like a luxury because, as a child, due to various Musicians' Union rules, recorded music was allowed to be played only at very specific times on the Light Programme (the forerunner of Radios 1 and 2). The only uninterrupted pop music was the chart rundown on *Pick of the Pops* every Sunday afternoon. This became essential listening, but there was also Radio Luxembourg, which broadcast in the evening from the Grand Duchy, and I often smuggled my radio up to the dormitory and listened with earphones late into the night. In the Sixties, I was swept along with this magic, which included the early careers of The Beatles and Rolling Stones. Perhaps the politics of the era, especially the Vietnam War, acted as a catalyst for some of the wonderful rock music being made, and I became obsessed. In the wake of The Beatles, and their unique melodic but simple pop songs, were other greats such as Bob Dylan, Jimi Hendrix, the Beach Boys, Led Zeppelin, and my own personal favourites, Traffic and Procol Harum.

All of this was going on to the backdrop of pirate radio stations playing records twenty-four hours a day, with the BBC playing hardly any recorded music until the launch of Radio 1 in 1967. Pirate radio was gold dust for a starved rock music fan, and it was a very sad day when Radio London was forced by the government to close down. As their final song they chose The Beatles' 'A Day in the Life', which ends with a forty-two-second piano chord that finally fades out., This moment was strangely moving.

My first interaction with anyone on the fringes of the music industry came through our favourite of my parents' friends, Laura Brand. She too had been caught up in the spirit of the 1960s and was unashamed to be slightly boastful about this. For us teenagers, she was speaking the same language, and she also had a wonderful sense of the absurd that made me and my siblings roar with laughter. She had hung out with the likes of Jimmy Page from Led Zeppelin and seemed to know all the cool people from swinging London. Her son Charles was also one of the few children of our parents' friends we liked having to stay, as he too had the music bug, his blue radio never leaving his side.

Later in my life, another strong musical influence on me was my friend Sophie's father Alex McEwen, who I got to know through spending New Year with the family in Scotland – a tradition that lasted for twenty-five years. Eck, as he was known, was a very talented guitarist and had toured America in the 1950s performing Scottish folk songs with his brother Rory, even appearing on the *Ed Sullivan Show*, on which The Beatles would make their legendary American TV debut a few years later. As a boy I had been ushered to the television by Nanny Nelson, who had a hawk-like skill of seeking out television appearances by aristocrats, to watch Eck and Rory on the early-evening current affairs programme *Tonight*.

Every New Year, Eck provided the musical centrepiece to the parties, and although he worked as a director of John Menzies in Glasgow to bolster the money supply, there was little doubt music was where his true passion lay. I got to sing on occasion, which perhaps boosted my confidence,

133

and there were always other musicians staying there, such as Richard Strange. Proudly socialist, Richard is very funny and brilliant with words. When I first met him, his band The Doctors of Madness was being hailed as the next big thing, but this ambition was kiboshed by the arrival of punk. We presented a rather unusual pair of duettists when we performed together as we are both over six foot six tall, and to this day we cross swords in regular Twitter spats.

In the 1970s, when I was in my early twenties, I had my first dalliance with becoming a rock star. Over the years I had developed a bit of a party piece, imitating the gravel-voiced white soul singer Joe Cocker, and I somehow ended up on stage with a band led by Bill Lovelady at a party. This received an uproarious response. I was a bit disappointed not to be asked to join them on a permanent basis, so I decided the time had come to form my own band, despite the fact that I couldn't play an instrument. It did seem, however, that Bill had taken note of me, and this was not the last time we collaborated together.

The band I formed was a ragbag of not particularly talented musicians, including my brother Eddie and a friend from Cirencester, Charlie Peile. We gave the band the rather odd name of Guzzling Porter – because I had seen a porter at Paddington Station swilling the contents of a whisky bottle – but we all took it incredibly seriously, even going through a Pete Best moment when Charlie was fired for not being a good enough drummer. We rehearsed in an air raid shelter in the Wimbledon garden of the parents of our guitarist James Todd, and everything was geared towards playing at his twenty-first-birthday party a couple of months later.

When the day came, we did a dress rehearsal that went reasonably well, but when the guests arrived, the room was crammed with people and, with the speakers being at floor level, the sound was completely blocked. It was a terrible moment when I sang the first line of our opening song, and virtually no sound came out. I sang myself hoarse to try to rectify the situation, but it was very disconcerting, and the band broke up shortly afterwards.

Several years later, Johnson, who by this time was working as a party DJ and had done some drumming with various musicians, called to tell me that Bill Lovelady was putting a band together and asked if I might be interested.

In 1979 Bill had a top-ten hit with his song 'Reggae for it Now', and his record company were ambitious to groom him for stardom. The one thing that he hates is relinquishing control, especially in this case where he felt his talents as a musician were not being respected. This reached the limit when he was told that before the next single came out, he should get his teeth fixed, and it was not long before he and the record label parted company.

Being very talented, Bill continued to carve out a career as a musician. He was popular in Sweden for some reason, and also worked on film scores, with particular emphasis on his classical guitar skills; one of his compositions was included in Prince Philip's funeral. I think perhaps part of him may have craved a bit more of the limelight. He therefore gradually put a band together comprising a hotchpotch of about fifteen vaguely talented amateurs he had noticed over the years, all of whom were delighted to bow to his far superior musicianship and join the project. I was invited to be one of the singers.

He called the band The Business, which seemed to give the right flavour for a collective of this nature. Unfortunately, it later turned out that the name had already been taken by a skinhead band with affiliations to the National Front and, as our fame grew, they started making aggressive public threats about us stealing their identity. We therefore decided to rebrand ourselves as The Business Connection, although I always felt this carried less weight.

I was one of the later recruits, and I don't know if it was by accident or design, but about half of the band members came from some of England's oldest aristocratic families: Johnson and I, Michael Cecil, Pickford Sykes, Valentine Lindsay and Theresa Manners, the daughter of the Duke of Rutland. Perhaps on the back of this we were asked to play at a charity function at the Hammersmith Palais, capacity in excess of two thousand.

With the looming Hammersmith Palais gig, we started rehearsing extensively, and Bill planned a show around our various skills. This involved the nucleus of the band playing on all the songs, but with guest appearances by vocalists such as Theresa and myself, as well as other musicians who Bill had come across over the years, such as a very eccentric-looking accordion player and a sitarist who was a cousin of Ravi Shankar. The whole thing presented a rather splendid spectacle.

There was quite a buzz and tickets sold out quickly. Bill decided we needed a manager and hired a slightly shady character universally known as The Rat. He was not in the music business but had close associations with some gossip journalists who were more than happy to give the event some extra advance publicity.

On the whole I don't suffer from stage fright, but I wasn't due to appear until about halfway through the concert, and therefore found myself alone backstage for about twenty minutes, and a feeling of sheer terror grew. Finally, it was my time and I stumbled on, slightly dazzled by the lights, and began to sing. My songs were the Joe Cocker version of 'A Little Help from My Friends' and a Steely Dan song called 'Do It Again', and it was marvellous to feel the audience respond to my performance as my voice echoed around the auditorium.

The real sensation was Theresa, who was a very attractive girl and made up for any limitations in her vocal skills with an extremely skimpy outfit and some truly wild dancing. The next day she was on the front pages of most of the tabloids comparing her to Madonna, who was probably the biggest star in the world at that time. The rest of the band, including me, were also favourably mentioned in dispatches and we really began to believe we were on to something.

Within days things started to happen. We were contacted by the nightclub impresario Peter Stringfellow, inviting us to play at his club, the Hippodrome. Stringfellow was a self-made man who had started his career running a small club in Sheffield, but by 1980 he had done well enough to take on the London market, first of all at Stringfellows in Covent Garden and later at the Hippodrome. He was an unquestionably tough businessman and proud of his northern roots, but his long hair, which caused him to resemble the pretty-boy rock star Peter Frampton from a distance, encouraged the deception that he was in it for the love of the music.

Stringfellow gave us a generous budget for the concert and, in addition to our already large numbers, we hired a gospel choir to do backing vocals. He also told The Rat that he must arrange maximum publicity, so there were endless photoshoots and interviews, and I would say we got more press coverage than Bruce Springsteen that summer. The concert once again was a total sell-out and the audience response even better than last time, the glamour quotient being massively improved by somebody persuading Mick Jagger to come along and see what all the fuss was about.

Our final song was Sly and the Family Stone's 'Dance to the Music', which gave every member of the band a chance to demonstrate their skills, and this was followed by a truly wild standing ovation for at least five minutes. As we left the stage I turned to Michael Cecil, son of the Marquess of Salisbury, and said I didn't think I had ever experienced anything like this. Michael seemed blithely unaffected and replied, in the incredibly upper-class voice shared by many of his family, 'As a former army officer I found being in Trooping the Colour more moving.'

Michael played saxophone and, while possessed of a wonderful sense of humour, was not cut from what might be called rock 'n' roll cloth. This had become evident at the very basic rehearsal studio we used, which had a small shop where you could buy soft drinks and crisps. One day Michael poked his head through the tiny shop window and, quite unembarrassedly, asked, 'Could I have a glass of champagne please?' He then seemed shocked to find that the drink in question was unavailable. Rather surprisingly, in later life Michael opted for an ex-pat existence in Kenya with his long-term girlfriend, Qiu Qiu, a very successful rave DJ from Beijing.

After this concert Stringfellow became convinced that the whole project could be developed further, believing that Theresa's glamour combined with the toff quotient in the band could, with the right material, have genuine hit-making potential. The headlines helped, including 'Right Royal Rock Up' and 'Top of the Toffs', many focusing on Theresa, such as 'Lady T's night of the garter', and 'Worcester's saucy scene' directed at me. He therefore signed a record contract with us, and I for one was convinced we were destined for stardom.

From this moment on, however, seeds of doubts were sown. Bill, who had formed the band because he wanted total control over his musical destiny, now found himself being edged out of the decision-making process by Stringfellow. I also had concerns that, although Stringfellow seemed keen to involve me, Theresa was the fish he really wanted to land, and I too might be cast aside. There was also the problem that Theresa's head had been turned by all the publicity and she was becoming increasingly difficult to work with.

It was something of a relief when it was decided that our first single should be Theresa and me doing a duet version of the Del Shannon classic 'Runaway'. The top producer Stewart Levine, who had worked with all sorts of artists including B. B. King, Simply Red and Lionel Richie, was hired. Although Stringfellow instructed him that his most important task was to showcase Theresa, he particularly liked my voice, and I got an equal input on the record, with my vocals perhaps dominating. He also incorporated a brilliant guitar solo by Bill, so he was happy as well.

I was delighted with the end result and remember playing it again and again at home with all sorts of dreams going through my head. It was therefore a moment of considerable disappointment when I received a call from The Rat saying that Stringfellow didn't like it and had found a more suitable song for Theresa to sing alone. The song was called 'Bring Me Down' and, while I know I was biased, it seemed like unutterable crap to me, but the band nonetheless recorded it and a marketing strategy was formed.

Stringfellow decided we should really go to town with the video for the single and hired the up and coming English director Bernard Rose to make it, giving him a budget of £50,000. Stringfellow had retained his Yorkshire accent and when we were discussing this plan he suddenly began talking about the various 'castles' families of the band members owned that might be suitable for the shoot, pronouncing 'castle' like the word 'tassel'. We went through the castle options provided by Theresa, Michael Cecil and me, and then someone mentioned that Pickford Sykes, whose father Sir Richard Sykes owned the Sledmere Estate, might also qualify. Stringfellow grew quite indignant: "E ain't got title, how come 'e's got cassle?'

Eventually we shot the video down in the legendary Hellfire Caves near Wycombe, where the Dashwood family had conducted all sorts of debauchery in the eighteenth century. The video had a very gothic feel, with whips and masks and Theresa performing suggestively around the rest of the band.

Before the single was released, we had a couple of gig commitments to fulfil, namely a charity party in the Albert Hall, followed by a Christmas concert at the Hippodrome. If

Stringfellow had pushed the boat out the first time, on this occasion he went berserk, and it was about as over the top as it could be. I enjoyed both events, but there was a slight feeling the magic was beginning to ebb away, not helped by the fact the endless press coverage was predictably becoming more hostile.

After the Hippodrome performance, Stringfellow called me, saying he wanted me to mime backing vocals at the launch party for the release of 'Bring Me Down'. I made a fuss about this as I was not even on the record, but he made all sorts of promises about the next single, so I went on stage and did it while feeling a bit of an idiot. He then insisted that Johnson and I accompany Theresa on a promotional tour of northern radio stations, which again held little appeal, but we dutifully went along. By this time relations between Theresa and the rest of the band had reached rock bottom. When she criticised something one of us had said in the first radio interview, Johnson snapped at her, whereupon she announced she was going back to London immediately. Needless to say, the remaining radio stations were rather disappointed the star had not turned up.

I think even Stringfellow must have realised the game was up, but the single was released and entered the charts at number 194, before dropping out the following week, after which it was fairly obvious the band could not continue in its current form.

It had always been my dream to front a band on my own

and after a short period of reflection, sometime in 1986, I started discussing with Bill the idea of putting a new line-up together. We decided to cut it right down to size, but to include some professional musicians, and within a few weeks we were rehearsing again.

Stringfellow was delighted and suggested that we have our comeback gig at the Hippodrome again, and we were also booked for a large charity party at Osterley Park in the presence of Princess Diana. As the rehearsals for the Hippodrome continued, Bill began to sense that, although the music was better, without Theresa the band lacked pizazz and needed that little extra something.

This all happened during the time I was first dating Tracy, and her *C.A.T.S.* co-star and friend Leslie Ash ended up being a key part of the band. Leslie's personality was a breath of fresh air. Something of a veteran in showbusiness terms, despite being only twenty-five, having been in a Fairy Liquid advert at the age of four, she had become every schoolboy's fantasy after her performance in *Quadrophenia* in 1979. Leslie was unembarrassed about adding another string to her bow when it was suggested she should take over Theresa's role in the band, for which her very powerful voice made her more than suitable, while also adding a sprinkling of stardust.

Come the day of the band's launch at the Hippodrome, we were quite confident, but things did not go to plan. Leslie had lost her voice a few days earlier and could not make the high notes, while I had to come to terms with the fact I could not carry the performance with my voice alone. The evening was a bit of a disaster and the press, who had for so long given us more publicity than we deserved, now relished the chance to dish out some payback, and they totally slated us. We played much better at the Osterley party, and according to a press cutting, Princess Diana agreed, but the damage was done, enthusiasm waned, and it looked like the end of another project.

One, seemingly final, chance to make it as a rock star emerged. Out of the blue I got a call from an American socialite, who had somehow got hold of one of our demo tapes and played it to the legendary boss of Atlantic Records, Ahmet Ertegun, who, having heard my voice, couldn't believe I wasn't black. A meeting was arranged with a top executive at Atlantic, who was enthusiastic but said he would be more interested if he could hear some original music written by the band. This was something we had never previously done, but the idea of trying appealed hugely.

In those days bands often used to set up a base deep in the countryside to inspire their creative juices, and this seemed a particularly attractive idea. The obvious place was Drynachan, the moorland shooting lodge overlooking the River Findhorn, which I had fallen in love with when staying with friends Emma and Liza Campbell. There is something about the big sky of Scotland, the way the

Findhorn can change from a gentle flow to a raging torrent overnight, and the fact, too, that it is miles from anywhere has always spoken to me. Renting it for a week, the band and I headed north into the wilds of Scotland.

We had the location, but only seven days to write our masterpiece. It could be said that we did not give the project maximum application as there was a general view that in being there, we should also live the rock 'n' roll lifestyle: one day was completely wasted on a magic mushroom trip. Nonetheless, we managed to make demos of five songs and returned south in a positive frame of mind. We then rented a recording studio, and I was really delighted with the finished product.

A lesson I have since learnt with regard to recording is that one has an inbuilt vanity about one's own voice, and while there was some merit in what we had done, with hind- sight it wasn't good enough to really excite a record company. Nonetheless, the rejection we received was disappointing, I never heard from Ertegun again.

Just before we went to Scotland, Stringfellow had one more roll of the dice and tried to wring some benefit from his association with us. He was opening a club in New York and flew Johnson and me out there. He put us up in a very smart hotel for us to attend the opening, hoping once again our aristocratic credentials could gain him some useful publicity. We were treated like rock stars, including a limou- sine picking us up from the airport, and after the opening spent a wild four days in the city, but the most significant event of the trip for Johnson was meeting Nile Rodgers and Steve Winwood. Johnson was beginning to harbour ambitions of becoming a record producer and really bonded with Nile, who told him he could arrange a job for him in a New York studio.

When we got home and were then turned down by Atlantic, Johnson decided that he would take up this offer. The idea of continuing the band without him, along with the feeling we had probably failed to hit the big time, made me slowly lose enthusiasm. The good news for Johnson was that not only had he discovered the career he wanted but also, in meeting Steve, he had found someone with whom he would enjoy musical collaborations right up until the present day.

I hadn't quite heard the last of Stringfellow. Twenty years later, after an all-male black-tie dinner, a group of us went on afterwards to his club, which he had now turned into an up-market lap dancing venue. I have never seen the point of lap dancing – the limitations on contact make the whole thing rather absurd – and the procedure is rather embarrassing. I was therefore planning to make a quick exit, at which point I heard Stringfellow's familiar voice: 'Hey Bunty, come over 'ere,' followed by instructions to three girls to look after me: 'Mandy, Molly, Daisy, this is Bunty, a great friend of mine. I want you to give him a really special time,' whereupon the girls either sat on my lap or gyrated wildly very close to my face. This generosity was the last thing I wanted. Out of courtesy I endured it for a while, before finally thinking the politest thing to do was to get a wad of £20 notes from my pocket and dole them out to the girls, then do my best to make as dignified an exit as possible.

After the demise of The Business Connection in 1986 my only live musical contributions were at functions such as the McEwen New Year, but my interest in rock music remained strong. Every Christmas Johnson and I used to make four CDs of the best songs of the year, and then listen to them reverentially over the holiday period. In the pre-iPod days, copies of these CDs were highly sought after, and we kept up the pretence that high security had to be maintained before the 'Track of the Year' was revealed. This joke became exaggerated when a girlfriend of Johnson's, the historian Lucy Moore, became rather persistent in questioning who the winner was. Johnson's surreal mind invented the idea that he had subsequently discovered her walking around, wired with a hidden recorder, hoping to pick up information about the identity of the champion.

I was quite surprised in the spring of 2002 to get a call from Valentine Lindsay, who had been the bassist in The Business Connection, saying that he had built a recording studio at his home near Cirencester, and was wondering if I would like to come over on Sunday and jam with him and some other musicians. I was not that enthusiastic, thinking that my rock days were over, preferring the prospect of watching the finale of an American golf tournament on television. His persistence eventually changed my mind. I became further enthused when I discovered that marijuana seemed to be the recommended fuel to fire the creative juices and, as we played, I suddenly felt the old pleasure of singing into a microphone coming back.

The personnel of the band kept changing every week in order to improve the sound, but we eventually settled on a line-up. As well as Valentine and me, there was Phil Legende, a drummer who had worked on the fringes of the music industry his whole life. His very long hair made sure everyone was aware of this. He also had the eccentric habit of wearing extensive make-up and women's clothes for live performances. There was Janet Thompson, an unassuming keyboard player who had played in a number of bands over the years and made her living as a music teacher. Then there was the guitarist, Hugh Dickens. The band was quite a mixed bunch, but nobody less matched the profile of a rock god than Hugh. A recently retired colonel in the army, he still had something of a military manner about him, with his short-back-and-sides haircut, his only concession to modernity being always to sport expensive dark glasses while playing. He did, however, have a style of playing the guitar that suited the band, and the songs that he had written, or 'ditties' as he chose to refer to them, somehow inspired my creativity to build lyrics and melody.

I can't quite remember why, but we decided to name the band Planet Potato. There was no logical reason for this, but it somehow portrayed the rather stoned framework around which the music was created and was also the name of one of our songs, for which I had had terrible trouble finding a word to rhyme with 'potato', eventually opting for the slightly unsatisfactory 'gazebo'.

Valentine, always an excellent organiser, booked us to play a gig at a local pub called The Tunnel. We were all quite nervous when the day of the gig dawned, and Hugh's wife tried to alleviate this by using a horsebox to transport our equipment, more akin to a Pony Club vehicle than the huge pantechnicons that ferry the Rolling Stones' kit from venue to venue. Nevertheless, the gig was a great success, with the crowd very forgiving of any minor blemishes, perhaps feeling an element of rapport for this unlikely group of people of a certain age risking looking ridiculous. News of our triumph spread, and we were asked to play Riffs Bar in Swindon, then the UK Music Pub of the Year. Riffs was owned by Andy Pett, who, together with his girlfriend Tiggy York, became members of my current band, The Listening Device. Our enthusiasm grew further when Valentine decided to bring two former colleagues from The Business Connection into the band, Bill Lovelady and Pickford Sykes, in a quest to further beef up the sound.

The real excitement came when Ned Lambton, the son of Tony Lambton (who lived in Italy with Tracy's mother), asked us to play at a party for his fortieth and his son Fred's eighteenth birthdays. We performed on the battlements of

Lambton Castle, a semi-ruin that belonged to Ned's family but had not been occupied since the 1930s. There were not only some high-profile people from the music business there, but it was also the most extraordinary party, fancy dress with some very wild costumes on display. There was the added bonus that Ned's father Tony had generously insisted that magnums of Lafitte should be placed on all the dinner tables, although some of the more conservative guests may not have totally appreciated the sight of drunken revellers staggering around late at night swilling this elixir from the bottle.

With Valentine and Janet also contributing to the writing, we had enough songs to record an album. The plan was to spend the winter in the studio and then launch it in London the following summer. In preparation for the launch of the album at Bush Hall, a 400-seater venue in London, we had a dress rehearsal for invited guests at Valentine's mother's house near Hungerford. Creating a stage in the garden, we hung a huge wooden sign with Planet Potato painted on to it. Things began well but suddenly, in a Spinal Tap moment, there came a noise from above and the sign crashed down on to the stage, grazing my back and only just avoiding what could have been a nasty accident.

Bush Hall was a success. We played to a packed house on a sweltering summer evening, fending off some slightly bitchy press about our age and so on. I wallowed in this fame for a few days, but about a week later I got wind of some sort of *coup d'état* taking place, with Hugh telling me that 'it had been agreed' that the band should now concentrate on doing more cover versions and playing wedding parties, with Bill taking over half of the vocal duties.

I felt hugely disappointed, unwilling to accept that this was the end of Planet Potato. Unlike in The Business Connection days, I had not expected we would become global superstars, but what I had really enjoyed was the creative process of writing and recording the songs. Perhaps because of this love for the process, Janet, Phil and I carried on writing songs on Janet's home recording equipment. Suddenly we found ourselves hitting new peaks of creativity, but the problem was that we still needed a band with which to unleash our brilliance on the world.

Phil knew a number of people on the fringes of the rock scene, and after one or two false starts on the personnel front we put together an operational band. The good thing about this new set-up was that, although Janet was very much the musical director, I was funding it, which meant that I could control the direction the music was going in, and in Janet I felt I had really found my musical soulmate.

We launched The Listening Device at the Half Moon in Putney, a small but legendary London venue where many famous bands had begun their careers, and gradually the rumour began to spread that we were not just dilettantes. Nonetheless, it was still a very pleasant surprise when we were asked to play at Highclere Rocks, a concert organised

by the Countryside Alliance, but where we would be support-
ing major artists including Eric Clapton, Roger Waters and
Bryan Ferry.

Later that summer Ned Lambton asked us to play again,
this time at his son Fred's twenty-first birthday at Cetinale.
Renting a huge tour bus complete with beds for the band
and equipment, I flew out with Tracy and the children, but
unfortunately the band had been busted at the border and a
small amount of marijuana confiscated. It might have been
a larger amount, but Phil could not bear to part with the rest
of his stash and chose instead to swallow it. Consequently,
Phil was not totally at the races during our set, but this was
generally perceived as being all part of the rock 'n' roll
experience.

Janet and I continued to write songs, and we then recorded
another album. We also played at some festivals, which was
very much more what I wanted to do rather than perform at
some of the more contrived gigs we had done with Planet
Potato. At the Glade Festival a problem arose when our
drummer Paul Holmes, who had just replaced Phil in the
band, rang up that morning and said he was suffering from
a serious bout of diarrhoea. Anyone who has been to a festival knows that this is the one place you don't want to suffer
from such an affliction, as lavatory facilities tend to be about
as basic as it gets. I therefore suggested that he literally come
in, play the gig, and then leave, hopefully not finding himself
stricken during the key period. From the lavatorial

perspective he successfully negotiated the problem, but he was late, and the general panic this caused meant that it was one of the worst performances musically that we ever gave.

We were invited by both Jools Holland and Bryan Ferry to support them at reasonably large venues when they were on tour, a major boost to band members' enthusiasm. Jools is a genuine renaissance man: not only is he one of the leading exponents of boogie-woogie piano in the world, but he has also fronted the BBC's long-running music show *Later* since 1992. In addition, he has strong cultural interests and will always visit interesting places or notable works of art wherever he is touring. This is reflected in the meticulous restoration of the house and gardens at Cooling Castle where he lives in Kent, home also to a huge train set that he has built up over the years, including carefully chosen models of real buildings that he has visited.

Jools has invited me on to the set of *Later* on a number of occasions, and on one of these, he had also asked a mutual friend, the rather unlikely figure of the landowner Philip Naylor-Leyland. Just as the show was about to begin, a technical problem brought a delay, and the audience was ushered into another room while this was dealt with. There we found ourselves slightly fish out of water, surrounded by what you might call bearded BBC types. Unfortunately, this was around the time of the pro-hunting rally in Parliament Square and, try as we might, everything we spoke of somehow seemed to return to this subject, causing some mildly disapproving glances from the rest of the crowd. Eventually Philip decided it was time to put a stop to our discussion and spoke quietly but firmly in my ear: 'Behind enemy lines, I think.'

It is a mark of Jools's wide-ranging interests that he maintains close friendships across an unusually broad spectrum, including aristocrats, musicians and other celebrities, not to mention his local publican, for whom he has deep affection. He is a good friend of Philip Naylor-Leyland's and told me that whenever he reaches any sort of crossroads where he cannot make a decision, he has a rule of asking himself, 'What would Sir Phil do?' I suspect he rather admires the rigid certainty with which Philip runs his life, but also enjoys the extremes of unintentional eccentricity that Philip shares with some other members of the aristocracy.

In 2005 Jools married Christabel McEwen, who he had been living with for sixteen years. I have known Christabel since she first arrived in London and married Ned Lambton a short time afterwards. She is excellent company and undoubtedly always the least selfish person in the room (perhaps something of a low bar with people like me around), which has caused her to be given the nickname of 'The Sainted One'. In recent years she has used this gift to become a highly respected child psychotherapist.

The wedding was awash with celebrities, including Paula Yates, who had been a co-presenter of the music show *The Tube* with Jools. She was not conventionally beautiful but incredibly sexy. I once sat next to her at a dinner of Jools's in

London and, by way of making conversation, she asked me what I did. I have never much enjoyed this question but mumbled some platitudes about owning an estate, and Paula suddenly interrupted: 'I bet you look fucking marvellous striding across your land.' While this was a slightly unusual reply, I couldn't help being rather pleased. It was very sad to witness the public downward spiral into which she descended following the death of her second husband, the rock musician Michael Hutchence, a few years later.

I was paid another rather unusual compliment by the film director Franco Zeffirelli. When he was in England, Franco spent a lot of time at the house of Maria St Just, who was the mother of two of my friends, Katya and Natasha Grenfell. He loved being surrounded by young people and, although I say it myself, I think he took rather a shine to me. One night, when we were all sitting and laughing around the dining room table, perhaps with the occasional spillage taking place, he suddenly announced in his flowing Italian accent, 'Bunter, I can see why the girls adore you. You are obviously noble, but you move like a lorry driver.' I would have to say that I was rather pleased with this description.

I sometimes come across Paula Yates's first husband, Bob Geldof. He is a man with a magnificent arrogance about him, and I was once at a dinner where someone suggested we play Trivial Pursuit. Bob responded enthusiastically and volunteered his services as quiz master. The only problem was that, as well as asking the questions, he insisted on answering them before anyone else had had a chance, which made for neither spectator nor participatory enjoyment.

Another time, I was sitting around with a group of people having a vaguely scientific discussion, and I made the point, which I don't think has ever been disproved, that life has never been created in a laboratory from nothing. Without malice, Bob roared into the conversation with, 'You feckin' eejit, it's happening all the time.' I felt it wasn't really worth continuing the discussion but couldn't help rather admiring the blind confidence with which he had interjected – he clearly enjoys a barney. His combative self-belief was, I'm sure, invaluable when he was putting Live Aid together.

Jools also introduced me to Mick Hucknall of Simply Red. Mick is definitely a political animal but, despite his blazing red hair, very much of the soft left, and I have had some interesting discussions with him. He is also a man who obviously enjoys good food and wine and, even when describing some romantic conquest from his past, he cannot resist a gastronomic metaphor such as, 'We were just getting down to the meat and potatoes of the situation.'

On the production front Johnson continued to work with a variety of artists, including on Bryan Ferry's album *Mamouna*, and this was the start of a working partnership that has continued sporadically to this day. Bryan is one of the most stylish people I know and an exceptional musician and performer, but his creativity thrives on friction. Every time he has started a new album there always seems to be a period when he and Johnson circle each other warily, both indicating they don't want to work together again, but at some stage they always seem to relent and the partnership resumes.

Another artist Johnson worked with was Peter Gabriel. Peter came to dinner one night at Badminton and his rather earnest charm went down well, but there was suddenly a crisis when it was announced that my father's dog Millie had run off. Panic ensued and the whole family rushed out into the park shouting endlessly but to no avail. After we returned, however, Peter suddenly quietly announced: 'I've got an idea.'

He walked out of the house and found a quiet spot on the edge of the park and began chanting in his very mournful voice, 'Millie, come to me Millie. Millie, come to me Millie.' This was a wonderful sound to hear resonating out into the night and I would love to be able to report that the dog suddenly bounded out of the darkness. Sadly, this was not the case, but she did reappear the next morning and may have simply appreciated spending the night outside, the air awash with these soothing vocals.

While my greatest passion was music, Tracy's was the environment, and she became an increasingly active campaigner in this arena. In the early days of our marriage, I encouraged these alternative interests, suggesting that were she to remain an actress it would take her away for weeks at a time, which could have a detrimental effect on

any children we might have. She took the idea of motherhood very seriously and was happy to go along with this.
We went on to have three children, starting with Bobby in
1989, followed by Bella in 1991 and Xan in 1995, and she
was, and continues to be, a devoted mother.

Just before Bobby was born, shortly after the discussion
where I raised my concerns about Tracy juggling acting and
motherhood, we were watching a programme on television
about green issues. Totally inspired, the next day Tracy
contacted the renowned environmentalist Teddy Goldsmith,
and together they concocted a plan for her to work at Friends
of the Earth, from where she could move on to greater things
if it proved a success. This seemed to tick all the boxes on the
marital front and provided a starting point for what became
an all-consuming passion and her life's work. Ironically, this
also created the single most important issue in the eventual
breakdown of our marriage years down the line.

CHAPTER 8

Poker and Politics

Studiously playing poker with my daughter Isabella.

BASED AT THE Cottage, Tracy and I still had a house in London, and while Tracy tended to stay at The Cottage, I split my weeks between town and country. Having quit MGL, I didn't pursue conventional work. Instead, I began to learn the runnings of the estate. Through regular meetings with the land agent Simon Dring and discussions with my father, the long process unfolded: the interconnected facets of finance, agriculture, law, housing, planning, forestry, sporting and hospitality, as well as getting to know the many characters who were tenants or working and living on the estate. But I continued religiously to spend a couple of nights in London and Wednesday evenings were reserved for poker.

I had hardly played poker since the 1970s, but Tim Hanbury had befriended Zac Goldsmith and both of them liked to gamble on almost anything. Zac suggested that Tim join the poker school he was involved with in London. In turn, Tim encouraged me to come along. I was a bit rusty to start with, but it was really enjoyable to meet a whole new group of people, all of them a deal younger than me, and Wednesday nights were firmly inked into my diary from then on. Interestingly, twenty years later, four of the game regulars became leading players in the political life of this country in the Boris Johnson era: Zac himself, Michael Gove, Ben Elliot and Dougie Smith.

· In those days Zac's principal political interest was environmental, as it probably still is now, but he was also very knowledgeable about the machinations of party politics and had little in common with the leftie fringe of the green movement. The Conservative Party was still very much in the doldrums and had gained the reputation of being 'the nasty party', so someone slightly alternative with Zac's good looks was exactly the sort of person it needed to recruit as an MP, and I think both Michael and Dougie were influential in nudging him in that direction. Since then, his political career has been a bit of a rollercoaster, but in Boris Johnson's government he was a Minister of State with the right to attend cabinet meetings and had a crucial role in implementing the government's green agenda.

Sitting down around the green baize with Michael Gove, as one tried to read the poker face behind those enormous glasses, reminded me of an early line in H. G. Wells's book *The War of the Worlds*: 'Human affairs were being scrutinised by minds immeasurably superior to our own.' At the time Michael was a journalist with a regular column in *The Times* and there was no doubting his intellect. This was not limited to just the political sphere. He also seemed to have a substantial knowledge of such diverse subjects as literature and rock music. He was also very good company, and the trademark courtesy that he exhibits in politics today was then very much in evidence, even amid the ruthless maelstrom of the card school.

Quite often, before the game, we would all have dinner together and politics were usually discussed. Other occasional attendees were podcaster and former cabinet minister, Rory Stewart, who did not actually play poker but came along for the political discussions with the young thrusters, and Kemi Badenoch, who went on to make serious inroads against better-known candidates in the 2022 Conservative Party leadership contest. Most of the group were Eurosceptics and, having heard his views on the subject, I was not surprised when, many years later, Michael Gove crucially sided with Boris Johnson in the referendum campaign.

Funnily enough I saw David Cameron at a dinner when he had just returned from Brussels in 2015 attempting to improve the terms of our EU membership, and I asked him whether he thought he could rely on Boris and Theresa May to support any agreement he managed to achieve. He dismissed the idea that May was a problem, before adding, 'Boris will be Boris.' Of course, the person I should have asked about was Michael, because Dave was definitely blindsided by what he saw as a betrayal when Michael threw in his lot with the Brexiteers, a decision that was probably pivotal to the final result. I could have warned him, with an element of certainty, that this was what Gove would do.

When I joined the poker school, Ben Elliot was just getting his concierge business, Quintessentially, going. Critical to the subsequent success was Ben's natural charm and easy way with people. As he became involved with the Conservatives it was this skill that made him such a good fit there as well. Under Boris Johnson, he became co-chairman of the party and, for a time, was very much in the inner circle. In 2023 he was knighted in Boris Johnson's controversial honours list.

Rather in the spirit of Anthony Powell's *A Dance to the Music of Time*, Ben is married to Steve and Genia Winwood's daughter Mary-Clare. He is also the cousin of Tom Parker Bowles – a food writer and son of Queen Camilla. A regular around our poker table, Tom tended to have a stream-of-consciousness style of play to match the humour and highly entertaining conversation he brought to the party.

Dougie Smith, a Scotsman who has been involved in politics all his life but shuns the limelight, is highly intelligent and advises the government on political strategy. He is married to Munira Mirza, who, despite having political origins on the left, went on to have a major job in Boris Johnson's government, described by him as one of the five most inspirational women he had ever met. Later on, however, she seems to have found Johnson's mode of government too erratic and she resigned in early 2022.

Dougie is above all a libertarian and was the co-founder of Fever Parties, an organisation that arranged orgies for young enthusiasts. It was all totally legal and non-profit making, and everyone who attended was very carefully vetted. There were strict rules: among others, men could not attend on their own, and no one over forty, of either sex, was admitted.

Some members of the poker school went along, but the age restriction meant that Tim Hanbury and I did not qualify. I was probably rather relieved by this, but Tim was determined to get his foot in the door. In the end Dougie relented and said that he could come as a barman. Tim was perhaps better suited to being on the other side of the bar, but I was fascinated by his description of how the evening evolved. To start with, people just stood around talking, as if it were some glorified cocktail party, but after about an hour there was suddenly some sort of unseen signal, and within seconds everyone's clothes were off, and wherever he looked all sorts of different shenanigans were going on.

The only trouble was that, like many a barman before him, Tim had indulged quite heavily in the product that he was dispensing, and as everyone now seemed to be otherwise engaged, he left his post and started wandering about. As he rounded a corner, he came across a naked man standing with an enormous erection, three girls at his feet worshipping and carrying out various acts of stimulation to the magnificent phallus. Tim blinked and then, before he had properly assessed the situation, cried, 'Eeoww Godd!' The man was naturally extremely displeased by this interruption, his splendid tumescence suddenly diminishing into nothingness. Needless to say, Tim was smacked with a lifetime ban from any future attendance.

I suppose it was not totally surprising that the press got wind of Dougie's involvement and the *News of the World* had a field day with stories of a top Tory spin doctor running orgies. Luckily, Dougie was given the heads-up from a journalist friend that the story was about to break. Rather cunningly he leaked it in advance to the matronly spinster MP Ann Widdecombe, who holds similar views about the permissive society to the much-ridiculed Mary Whitehouse. When she predictably made a terrible fuss about it, there was rather more sympathy from the liberal establishment than there might otherwise have been. David Cameron was by now leader of the Conservatives and decreed that Dougie could keep his job, but sadly this was conditional on his desisting immediately from his involvement in Fever Parties.

In interviews he gave at the time Zac had admitted that he was 'not a monk' and that his principal vice was gambling. This perhaps encouraged Aspinalls casino to let us hold our poker games in their private rooms, as Zac himself was a relatively high roller and his general charisma encouraged other high-profile people to join our evenings, which was good both for casino takings and for the general image of the club. These visitors included Shane Warne, Kate Moss, Trudie Styler and Lennox Lewis, as well as other fairly heavy punters such as Taki and David Tang.

I sometimes suspected that Shane's main reason for attendance was the probability of finding some pretty girls there, but he was actually a good poker player. In fact, he had a clause in his television commentary contract that, if he should reach a final of a major poker tournament, then he could pull out of commentary duties for any cricket match on at the same time. The other thing surprising in such an elite athlete was that he seemed to chain-smoke along with the rest of us without damaging his sporting prowess. It was a terrible shock, then, when he died in 2022.

We were greatly excited when Kate Moss came along, as she possesses a rather wonderful gift, perhaps a key ingredient of her modelling career, of being able to be slightly flirtatious simultaneously with everyone in the room. She is also reputed to have perfect recall about people she has met. As it happened, I had met her once before in Ibiza and this created a rather embarrassing moment. We were playing poker at a circular table with a large metallic light directly above, shining down so people could see their cards. I happened to be sitting directly opposite an open door, beyond which was a long passage leading to the top of the stairs. A girl appeared from the stairs and began walking down the passage as if it were a catwalk and, as she approached the door, I recognised Kate. As she got closer, she seemed to be looking at me and, as she drew closer still, I suddenly realised that she was heading directly towards me to say hello.

While this was obviously good news, it also came as a bit of a shock, and I leapt out of my chair totally forgetting about the overhead light. There was a terrible clanging noise as my head struck it, causing it to swing from side to side and nearly knocking me out. Kate made a quick judgement call and swerved away at the last minute, not wishing to accost this cartoon character with stars swirling around his head, but I rather felt as if I had missed a trick.

Trudie Styler is not that much younger than me but still looks extremely good, perhaps an endorsement of the tantric sex that she and her husband Sting have publicly espoused over the years. She is much more than your average rock wife, however, and has successfully produced several quality films, as well as campaigning for many humanitarian causes. She always seemed to enjoy her poker sessions, describing us all as 'my boys'.

For a man whose profession was violence, Lennox Lewis was a surprisingly placid, but more than competent, poker player. He would spend quite a long time looking at his cards but then had an incredibly cool way of flicking a chip into the air and making it land in exactly the right place on the table. He was introduced to the game by a 25-stone Nigerian called Ade, a great friend of Ben Elliot. Ade had a finger in many pies, including being an occasional actor, having appeared as an African prince in one of the gambling scenes in *Casino Royale*, as well as playing the getaway driver who gets stuck in the car door in the Guy Ritchie film *Snatch*.

Playing poker with all of these characters meant that political changes felt very close to home. Ever since my time at Cirencester, I have read magazines such as the *Spectator* and the *New Statesman*, developing a lifelong interest in politics, albeit on an armchair basis. As well as being fascinated by the machinations of politics, at the back of my mind there is always the worry of how any dramatic changes might affect Badminton and all of us who live and work there.

Back in the 1970s my father and I watched the left-wing agenda unfold, espoused by Tony Benn, but also by Chancellor Denis Healey, who threatened to 'tax the rich until the pips squeaked', both of us worrying that it would spell the end of the line for Badminton after half a millennium. Possibly the most life-changing event of this period was the election of Margaret Thatcher in 1979. Prior to this, even when the Conservatives had been in power, it was a reasonable assumption that it would be very difficult to either maintain the Badminton estate or live in the house during my lifetime. When Mrs Thatcher embarked on her very daring agenda, it transformed the country. Thirty years on, it still plucks at the heartstrings to watch footage of her resignation. She was a controversial figure, but I still feel that without her Britain would have simply continued on an inexorable socialist decline.

Our poker nights continued as David Cameron came to the fore. His rise was aided by Michael Howard delaying his resignation following his defeat in the 2005 election, allowing the young thrusters, Cameron and George Osborne, to make their mark. Dave Cameron's mother-in-law, Annabel Astor, has always loved a bit of behind-the-scenes scheming, and became concerned that the ambitions of the family protégé might be thwarted by the even younger pretender Osborne. When I went to stay at her house for the weekend, I therefore took as a house present the DVD of the brilliant BBC series *I, Claudius*, in which Livia, the sinister wife of the Emperor Augustus and mother of his possible heir apparent Tiberius, poisons anyone who threatens her son's ascension to the top job. Annabel quickly squirrelled it away in the bottom of her desk, doubtless planning to study this blueprint in detail when all the guests had left.

Dave, of course, did get the job, and probably the main event during his period as opposition leader was the global financial crisis of 2008. I listened to this unfold, sensing that things might never be the same again. By 2010, when the Labour Party was finally ousted from power, it was quite strange to be able to say that one knew the new Prime Minister. In some ways I think David Cameron was initially quite surprised to find himself in such an elevated position.

When I saw him shortly after the election, he recounted a story of his meeting Barack Obama in fairly star-struck terms, and how he had told Samantha that she had best make the most of their trip on Air Force One as it would probably never happen again. At least in the short term, his premiership will be judged by the Brexit referendum of 2016, which led to his downfall. This does not do him justice and to my mind he was on many fronts one of the better prime ministers of my lifetime.

Dougie Smith was very impressed with how Dave never panicked in a crisis, and it must be said that he did possess the invaluable asset of not going slightly mad in office, unlike some of his predecessors. I'm sure he was helped here by having Samantha as his wife, who kept him grounded and insisted on regular family time taking place, however busy he was. She also added a trendy dynamic to their relationship, which encouraged some wag to christen them 'Sam and Dave', after the famous Sixties soul duo of 'Soul Man' fame.

One can't quite envisage Gordon Brown or Theresa May giving a party like the one I attended at Chequers, which turned into a wild rave with Ibiza DJs. The party was billed as a belated fortieth birthday for Samantha and comprised about two hundred people who were glad to indulge in the sort of behaviour they had enjoyed at university about twenty years earlier, and they dressed and behaved accordingly. Dancing was in the Great Hall and the DJ was an Ibiza regular called Sarah HB. Cameron paid for the party himself but there was still some criticism from Labour MPs that government buildings should not be used for private functions of this nature, although I would think the whole business gave him more political credit than the unfortunate image of his opposite number, Ed Miliband, struggling with a bacon sandwich a few days later.

The party took place shortly before the 2015 election, probably because Dave knew it might be the last chance to hold it there, but he once again confounded the odds and won an overall majority, and it looked as if his plan to retire on his own terms a few years later would come to fruition.

I met Boris Johnson in 2014, when he was still mayor of London, shooting grouse in Northumberland. I don't know if he was telling the truth, but he claimed never to have shot grouse before and then proceeded to display a phenomenal degree of marksmanship for a beginner. Our host was a strong believer in Brexit and was already beginning to woo politicians he thought might support the cause, although at this stage Boris had not declared himself either way. As one would expect from his public persona, Boris was very entertaining and exhibited an obvious intelligence. He also displayed a predictable confidence about Conservative chances in the forthcoming election, although I did note in my diary that a slightly roguish look was never far from his face. Nonetheless, having listened to him being questioned by the assembled guests, I left the weekend favourably inclined to his potential, not least because he was the antithesis of modern-day politicians who are generally presented in a totally choreographed way.

Although I had voted unhesitatingly to join the EU in 1975, as time went on, I had become rather disillusioned with it, irritated with the way it had become a bloated bureaucracy telling us to do things that we were perfectly capable of making our own mind up about. When it came down to it, I decided that the trade benefits and general maintenance of the status quo outweighed this annoyance, and reluctantly voted to remain in the 2016 referendum. It was interesting how my friends, who tended to be Conservative voters, exhibited no obvious signs of which route they favoured, with husbands and wives quite often voting the opposite way.

Over this period, I came across a number of key players in the Brexit story. I met Nigel Farage when he was a guest at a Brexit celebration dinner that Robin Birley was hosting in his club, 5 Hertford Street, which we somehow stumbled into, while not actually feeling there was much to celebrate. He rather lived up to his image, swilling drink and chain-smoking as he held court, and I must admit he was quite charming in an awful sort of way. While not exactly a politician, he can be regarded as a brilliant activist in that, more than any other single person, he must be credited for achieving Brexit. I couldn't help thinking, however, that he was essentially a destructive force who knew what he *didn't* want, while lacking a clear vision of exactly what he would replace it with.

About a week later I went to the annual *Spectator* party. Theresa May was there and, as frontrunner for party leader, was in great demand. Even from a distance it was obvious that she was loathing all the attention and would have been far happier back behind her desk; her only concession to social interaction was an uncomfortable laugh in which her shoulders heaved up and down, rather in the manner that Ted Heath had made famous many years earlier.

After he lost office, I often came across David Cameron at various functions. There was no doubt that he was bruised by his Brexit experience, but he is well adjusted and unlike, for example, Margaret Thatcher, had a life to fall back on outside politics. He came to stay at Badminton the week before the 2019 election. Constantly in touch with the pollster Lynton Crosby, he was certainly as hopeful as anyone that his nemesis Boris Johnson would be successful, for all their past differences. I suppose, in terms of his legacy, the subsequent victory at least meant that the whole business of Brexit has not resulted in an extreme socialist government.

CHAPTER 9

Shooting Stars and the Fat Cat Four

Practising golf in the park at Badminton.

A MAJOR BENEFIT of not being tied to conventional employment was that I was able to indulge an obsession of my own: golf. Here I must make an appeal to my readers not to turn away at the mere mention of this word, although I do understand that for some the prospect is about as exciting as watching paint dry. In requesting your indulgence, I would add that I do not propose to go into detailed descriptions of the game, but more to explore the range of emotions, from extremes of laughter to the depths of agony, that I have derived from it, and to explain that there is a mysterious correlation between golf and life itself.

Ever since my teenage years I have adored the game but shown very little natural aptitude for it. Even for a player of my limited skills, however, just occasionally one hits a shot that Tiger Woods himself would be proud of, and this unleashes an almost orgasmic surge of pleasure; my brother Johnson, rather too scientifically, describes this as the 'spermatozoa moment'. When one returns to more mundane, or even disgraceful, standards, the misery feels as intense, but luckily the sight of one's opponents suffering similar travails can quickly restore happiness and general mirth.

The main focus of my golfing endeavours is the annual tournament I started at Stinchcombe Golf Club in 1988, and which continues to this day. It involves about sixty players paying a large entrance fee, pooled to create a huge cash prize for the winner. This prospect creates enormous pressure, possibly akin to that suffered by professionals in the Masters. It has become a deeply personal quest to win this tournament.

It could even be argued that this obsession had an indirect effect on British political history. In 1997 I volunteered to go canvassing for David Cameron, when he was standing for parliament for the first time at a seat in Stafford. I had met Dave a year earlier, staying with William Astor and his wife Annabel, who is Samantha Cameron's mother, and, even then, it was obvious he had the potential to go right to the top. I was therefore quite excited to go and stay with the Camerons at their cottage in the constituency for a few days and help out.

Canvassing brings one into contact with people from all sorts of different backgrounds going about their lives. My experience also included moments of terror: fearsome dogs leaping up to the window or trying to bite one's fingers while I stuffed literature through the letter-box. The whole business of letter-boxes was in itself a bit of a learning curve: I had not realised so many were at ground level, and being 6 foot 6, I cut a rather absurd figure having to kneel on the doorstep to push the stuff through.

There was also time for moments of fantasy. Occasionally the door would be opened by a rather scantily clad woman giving off a hint of availability, and momentarily I would be transported into a scene from the 1970s film *Confessions of a Window Cleaner*. We were actually instructed not to get into detailed discussions about policy, but one woman was particularly insistent, haranguing me about what the Conservatives were going to do about VAT on pensioners' winter heating oil, and as I didn't know the answer to the question I just stood there rather vacuously, eventually suggesting they should 'wrap up warm'. Dave by this time was observing from nearby and asked me what had happened; when I explained, a flicker of concern crossed his smooth countenance.

All canvassers were presented with large blue rosettes to wear and there was quite a lot of time spent hanging around while Dave delivered detailed policy explanations. With the Stinchcombe tournament only a week away I began using these moments to practise my golf swing, at first gently but gradually progressing into full-blooded efforts, which in my mind's eye constituted top-quality play.

My dreams were interrupted by the constituency agent rushing up in a rather agitated state, requesting I desist immediately from this activity. I emerged from my trance and suddenly realised that a group had gathered to watch my display, and the fact I was wearing the blue rosette left no doubt about my political persuasion. When they saw me being reprimanded there were guffaws of laughter from the assembled crowd, and I think I can say with a degree of certainty that I did little for the cause of caring conservatism on that day.

Dave's bid for parliament ended up being swept away by the Blair landslide of 1997 but I fear that my efforts did little to encourage people wanting to defy the trend and vote for a strong local candidate.

I didn't win that year's tournament and sadly, thirty-five years on from its conception, this ambition remains unfulfilled. It endures, though, and on the night before the tournament I am like a child on Christmas Eve, totally unable to sleep, though in an unchildlike way I then resort to a sleeping pill.

Every year I send out an invitational letter to all contestants, which, although I say it myself, encompasses some of the highest echelons of golfing humour. The night before the event, there's the 'Fork Supper'. I had never heard of the term 'fork supper' until it was coined by Guy Morrison. The definition is 'food that is served on one plate and eaten with just a fork', which I don't think does justice to the lavish feast that is served in the North Hall. The supper is washed down with vast amounts of claret, although it is noticeable that the more ambitious players hold back a bit. Others, drunk with the fantasy of winning, place all sorts of bets that they regret the following morning.

When the tournament is finished, we gather around the clubhouse for the presentation of a shield of unfathomable commonness, with engraved names of previous winners, together with 'the green jacket', which, just as in the Masters at Augusta, is slipped on to the shoulders of the winner by the previous year's champion.

Speeches then follow, although the standards of oratory exhibited by the players tend to be fairly modest, but one year someone in the assembled audience shouted at the victor, 'Hey Dick, what are you going to spend the money on?' Dick, who was about to pocket in excess of £8,000, delighted the crowd by replying, 'I'm going to put it all up my nose.' This witticism caused whoops of delight and was repeated many times in various salons and clubs of London, to such an extent it got back to Dick's father. By this time the story had become rather jumbled, and his father anyway had no idea why he would want to put a lot of money, or anything else for that matter, up his nose, so he assumed his son was planning to have some sort of nasal reduction surgery. He took him aside and gently tried to dissuade him: 'Look here old boy, we've all got quite big conkers in our family, but I really wouldn't waste all that money on a silly operation like that.'

Various celebrities have played in the tournament, most

famous being Hugh Grant, who won in 2003. When I first met Hugh, he was even worse than me at the game, which can be translated as meaning he was an extremely bad player. He became obsessed, however, and had lessons and practised a great deal whenever he wasn't acting, and quickly made a substantial improvement. He likes to give off a laid-back air, but I suspect he adopts a similarly intense dedication when preparing himself to get into character for an acting role.

The year I came closest to winning I was in the final afternoon group, paired with two veterans, the actor Michael Medwin, a stalwart of the British film industry in the 1950s and 60s, and Sunny (the Duke of) Marlborough. Sunny complained constantly that he was suffering from terrible 'collywobbles' from the previous night's dinner, almost indicating he thought the tournament should be postponed to accommodate this ailment, and his challenge faded early on. Medwin on the other hand, who was by now in his eighties, showed a single-minded determination that I have never seen on a golf course, and took the honours almost by strength of will alone. He continued playing golf until shortly before his death at the age of ninety-five and I'm sure this discipline prolonged his life.

Sunny also devoted a very high level of concentration to golf, but this came at the price of not speaking at all during a round. One year, my friend John Parry was drawn to play with him, unaware of this trait, and during the early holes tried unsuccessfully to make polite conversation. Sunny barely grunted but John gently persisted, making a comment on the sixteenth hole that it looked as if there might be some rain coming. This finally did garner a reaction, as Sunny studied the weather assiduously every morning. 'You bloody fool,' he responded contemptuously, 'when the wind comes from the west it's bound to blow the clouds up the River Severn,' before slumping back into silence for the rest of the round. His prediction proved correct.

When my obsession with the tournament was at its zenith, I thought it would be amusing to have a £50,000 car as the prize for anyone getting a hole in one on the ninth hole. I arranged this with the local Audi dealer, but they insisted I take out an insurance policy costing nearly £1,000 against someone actually achieving the feat. The car was then placed by the hole and a representative from Audi stood there as referee for the entire morning. Nobody won the prize, and he reported back to me that only nine out of the sixty players had actually landed their ball on the green, let alone see it drop into the hole.

I have always been fascinated by the game's ability to bring players' inner torments to the surface, and this was never more evident than with a group of my golfing friends christened the 'Fat Cat Four', because of our ability to find the time and money to enjoy the game in all sorts of exotic locations. The others in this group were Philip Naylor-Leyland, Rob Hesketh and Matthew Dugdale.

Philip, on first meeting, perhaps comes over as rather conventional and rigid, which is why it was amusing to be with him on the set of *Later . . . with Jools Holland*, but underneath lurks a splendidly eccentric sense of humour. He was originally disdainful about golf and took it up only in order to play in a competition at his son's school. But from that moment he got the bug. I think the precision of the handicapping system appealed to his cerebral side, as he could monitor any improvement or decline in his play with a degree of exactitude, but he is also prone to dropping any semblance of rectitude and letting out the most extraordinary noises when he makes a really bad shot; one of his variations sounds rather like a kettle as it approaches boiling point. He also understands the humour of the game and is often to be found reading P. G. Wodehouse's golfing stories and suddenly exploding into bellows of genuinely manic laughter.

'Philip's gone to America to stare at golf courses,' once declared his wife Isabella, a characteristically inscrutable look on her face. She'd been rather confused by his sudden passion for the game, and it now turned out he was using an American trip to recce locations for a future golf holiday. She did perhaps have some cause for genuine concern: Philip was going through a stage of bursting into paroxysms of laughter whenever golf was mentioned. On a more soothing note, she sometimes found him becalmed in an almost Zen-like trance when reading a book called *Golf in the Kingdom* about the spiritual aspects of the game.

Matthew Dugdale is a man of considerable bulk and undoubtedly the most powerful hitter in this group. Unfortunately, he lacks directional skills when applying this talent and, although possessed of a fine intellect off the course, is incapable of utilising any cerebral skills on it, sheer bombastic power being the only part of his armoury that he can apply with any degree of regularity. On one occasion I was playing in a mixed doubles competition with him when his partner was injured and had to be replaced at the last minute by the club pro's wife. We teed off and Matthew gave his ball a fearsome swipe, sending it into the middle distance, but unfortunately to an area of the course that had not seen human traffic in a generation. This caused his bespectacled partner to stare aghast for a few moments, and then comment in a strong Birmingham accent, 'Flippin' 'eck.'

Under normal circumstances Matthew's lack of golfing prowess should have been translated into an increase in his handicap, but he has an irresistible desire to boast about even modest improvements in his game, so we resolutely resist any change in his handicap at all costs. His fellow golfers feel that he would become unbearably odious if a handicap adjustment allowed him to win more often and so we have refused to budge, and are rewarded as the course reverberates every time he hits the ball with his signature cry of, 'Oh for God's sake . . . Oh for God's sake.'

Rob Hesketh has now sadly died but his favourite brand

of humour was *schadenfreude*, which the game of golf provided endless opportunities to indulge. He was a fairly quiet man, but with a sly wit, and one could almost sense a purr of delight emanating when someone struck a bad shot. This was particularly applicable when the exponent of the shot was Matthew, who, although probably his best friend, provided additional enjoyment because there was some-times an inevitability about his explosions of poor play.

Just before he died, Rob started a two-day tournament that took in some of the great courses on the Lancashire coast. His wife Catherine decided to continue with it in his honour after his death, a very popular decision as we could consequently not only remember our departed friend, but also partake of the top-of-the-range wine cellar he had built up. This might explain why there always seems to be a 100 per cent acceptance rate for this tournament, while Stinchcombe hovers around 60 per cent.

The spiritual aspect of golf may have been in evidence during the first tournament after Rob's death. After day one Philip had what seemed like an unassailable lead, with me a distant second. I like to think that when my body was suddenly taken over by almost superhuman golfing skills it was perhaps Rob guiding it from on high, while the impec-cable standards that Philip had displayed the previous day plunged into decline, and the 'kettle' noise evolved into something like a wounded water buffalo.

Another 'major' is the Welsh Open, when I always stay with Guy and Penny Morrison, who host the tournament at a course near their house in Wales. As with Stinchcombe, large cash prizes are on offer and I'm glad to announce that I once stood on the victor's rostrum there. Thrilled, I was covered with goose bumps about four holes from the finish as I realised, if I kept my nerve, I could be lifting the trophy aloft.

The inaugural year of the Welsh Open was in 1992 and took place two days after the fortieth birthday party I had shared with the successful novelist Hannah Rothschild, who is ten years younger to the day than me. The party was held at the newly opened Ministry of Sound, where we danced extensively until dawn. The next day I drove down to the Morrisons' place, where there was another late night, followed by two rounds of the golf competition and a post-match party the following day. Even by my hedonistic standards this was a demanding schedule, and at a barbecue lunch on Sunday I suddenly felt incredibly dizzy on lighting a cigarette, sweat pouring down my face. I really thought I might be having a heart attack and was taken upstairs, where I lay on the bed, soaking the pillow with sweat. There was some concern, and a doctor was summoned, but by the time he arrived I was feeling a little better. The conclusion was that I had just had a bit of a turn, brought on by general excess. This provoked some wag to climb on to the balustrades of the house where we were lunching and formally announce, 'The Marquess will live,' followed by cheers of delight from the assembled crowd. It was a bit of a wake-up call and from that moment on I modified my drinking and gave up my forty-a-day cigarette habit.

Golf holidays have taken me all over the world, including to Thailand, where there are some wonderful courses, but the weather there tends to be very hot and humid. All the caddies are women, presumably because there is some cultural perception that it is a demeaning job for a man to do.

Thai women are, in the main, extremely small, which makes it all the more remarkable that they are capable of carrying enormous golf bags around in the heat, but I was particularly surprised one day when my caddie, who must have been under five foot tall, pointed up at my 6-foot 6-inch frame and announced, 'You very tall.' I politely acknowledged this fact, but she continued her observation by saying, 'Me very small.' Once again, I could only agree with this statement, but I wasn't quite ready for her follow-up remark: 'Is very good 'cos me can go . . .' – and then she simulated oral sex with her hand and mouth. I didn't know how to react, but I felt relieved that the male caddies at Sunningdale do not offer similar services.

America is of course the ultimate golfing destination, and I used to combine a riotous few days in New York City with a trip to the Hamptons, Long Island, where there are a number of magnificent and very exclusive golf clubs. This tournament became known as The International for the obvious reason that the participants were based on both sides of the Atlantic. One of the courses was the Maidstone Club, which maintains some rules of behaviour and etiquette more appropriate to the nineteenth century. Our host, the successful property developer Chris Clark, who sadly died in 2020, was on the one hand quite pleased to introduce an English aristocrat into these surroundings. On the other, he was permanently on his guard, aware that places exhibiting any form of pomposity tend to bring out the worst in me, and he put his head into his hands when, on one occasion, I was unable to staunch a gentle but persistent flow of expletives.

Our golfing group has comprised quite a mixed bag of competitors, including both Roger Waters of Pink Floyd and the Bad Company drummer Simon Kirke. Like many a self-respecting rocker, Simon has done a stint in rehab, and this happened to coincide with Tiger Woods's spell in the same facility for sex addiction. They became good friends, and it was a treat for the patients to gather round and watch the Golf Channel while Tiger provided expert commentary.

Simon and other inmates were once listening in awe to the great player expounding on his subject when another patient entered the room almost in tears and announced, 'Oh my God, I've just heard my dog died. I don't think I can take it. I'm gonna have to start using again.' This was obviously a mildly annoying interruption, but one man took it more seriously than the others, turning around and shouting, 'I don't give a fuck about your bloody dog; we're listening to Tiger talking about golf.'

I happened to be on a golfing holiday in the Hamptons a month after 9/11 and I was fascinated by the American reaction. There were flags everywhere, both on buildings and on cars, and I spoke to some normally sophisticated people at dinner parties who said they felt completely violated, and that from now on, as far as they were concerned, any Muslim was the enemy. Everyone was very jittery, and I remember one of the Americans on the golf trip suddenly ringing his wife and saying he didn't want his children going back to the city for the foreseeable future.

I also went to a party, organised jointly by American *Vogue* and the TV music channel VH1, to raise money for families of firemen killed when the buildings collapsed. During the auction the audience went crazy for about ten minutes, chanting 'USA . . . USA,' but quickly lost concentration when the auctioneer tried to explain what would happen to the money that was raised. It was also noticeable that all the firemen who were actually there had become babe magnets in a way not seen since British soldiers returned on home leave in England during the Second World War. I had gone to the party with Seb Lee, a friend from the poker school in London now living in New York, and he happened to be wearing an expensive blue shirt that was a similar colour to the firemen's shirts; persistently, and possibly a fraction reluctantly, he had to turn down the advances of hordes of these newly patriotic women.

Another regular golfing venue was Cape Town, a trip organised by Fat Boy Coltman-Rogers, who now lived almost full time on his Welsh estate, so this provided the chance of a rare sighting of him. He had come to golf fairly late in life but was a natural athlete, and his swearing pedigree found the perfect outlet in the game. Another expressive player was Margaret Thatcher's son Mark, who was a first-rate golfer but not brimming with charm. His mother's voice was of course recognisable, possibly modified by elocution lessons, but Mark had deliberately turned his back on her manner of speech and adopted what might be termed a hardcore estuary accent. This was particularly evident when he sent a long putt heading towards to the hole and he would shout, 'Get in the bucket, get in the bucket,' in a mildly unattractive way.

One year I was invited to play in the pro-am section of the Dunhill Masters. I was in a team captained by Mark O'Meara, who had won the Masters and the British Open that year, and another team member was Prince Andrew. One way and another, we had quite a large crowd following us round the course. I don't know if it had anything to do with this, but I played the best golf of my life, certainly relishing the cheers as I miraculously hit ball after ball to within six inches of the hole.

The night before the game we were given dinner by the

Dunhill chairman and, while not wishing to kick a man when he's down, I was not much charmed by Prince Andrew. He seemed a dull man and assumed we were interested in the quantum mechanics of golf club design or detailed technical aspects of his work in the Navy. He also made some rather heavy-handed attempts at humour, followed by guffaws of laughter, interspersed with some very bland stories about 'Mother'. In his defence, it must be hard for anyone in his position to develop judgement about what is interesting or amusing when there is no shortage of toadies around every corner telling him what a fascinating person he is.

That lack of sound advice may have been a contributing factor to his involvement in the Epstein/Maxwell scandal. Some years earlier I found myself next to Ghislaine Maxwell at a couple of dinners in London. She was easy enough company, but the extraordinary thing was that she was obsessed to a degree I have never known before or since by her father, Robert Maxwell. At the time he was a media tycoon rivalling Rupert Murdoch, and Ghislaine brought every topic back to some reference about him.

Golf has always provided an excellent bonding mechanism with my family. My father enjoyed the game more than he cared to admit, and most weekends Johnson and I used to play with him. On the course he tended to assume everyone knew who he was and adopted a rather ducal air, politely saying 'good morning' and 'how are you?' to everyone. In reality the golfing world and Badminton over-lapped less than he thought, and he was not instantly recognised.

Nowadays I play a lot of golf with my two sons, both of whom are substantially better than me, but it is very competitive. There is much betting, which for some reason I usually seem to lose, and most years we incorporate a gastronomic trip to a golfing destination abroad in our schedule. They and indeed some of their contemporaries have a slightly annoying habit of filming some of my worst play and then posting it on Instagram, and the contortions of rage and bad language I occasionally exhibit have caused these films to go viral. With computer literacy and command of social media not being my strong suits, my revenge will have to be served cold.

Meanwhile my father's restless nature meant that he always liked to have a project on the go. These included restoring Swangrove, a house in the woods that had been built by the 3rd Duke for his mistress, to a modern-day version of its former glories. He also designed a large circu-lar swimming pool with a fountain in the centre in the garden at Badminton. The project that was a constant work in progress, however, was the shoot at Badminton.

Master once took me out in his Land Rover and, stopping it by some pheasants eating corn in a nearby field, suggested I shoot one of them. I was a bit surprised at being entrusted with what seemed a slightly unsporting task, but fired nevertheless and was surprised to discover I had missed it completely. This was inevitably followed by the familiar refrain: 'You *stupid* boy.'

Despite his interest, he considered shooting the poor relation of fox-hunting, and was frightened that even the smallest attempts to improve the shoot in the park might threaten the quality of his favoured sport. My father gave up hunting shortly after Master's death and shared no such qualms, starting initially with improvements to the existing shoot, but then moving it on to areas on the more hilly outskirts of the estate where the topography was more suitable.

From then on, my father strove constantly to make it better, and, every time I returned from a weekend staying with friends who owned high-quality shoots, his first question was, 'Is it as good as ours?' To start with I had to qualify my answers, saying it was not really comparable, but as time went on there was no denying that, through constant experimentation, he had created one of the great shoots in the country.

I think he enjoyed shooting but not excessively, his main interest being this quest for improvement. It meant that developing the shoot became a progressively more expensive hobby, so he decided to have two or three weekends in the year where overseas guns would pay for two days of top-quality shooting The shooting guests would stay in the house and he would bring his chef from London down especially for these occasions and serve the very best wine from his cellar.

There was a group of proudly Republican Texans and their wives who used to come every year. One time their visit coincided with the 'dangling chads' election of 2000 between George W. Bush and Al Gore, where the whole thing came down to a few votes in Florida and required endless recounts. After the first day's shooting my father received a call from the gamekeeper saying that some additional birds had been picked up and could be added to the bag, but when he came into the room and announced, 'Good news, they've found another forty,' everyone assumed that he was talking about votes, and he was temporarily surprised by the uncharacteristic hooting and hollering that this news caused among the guests.

A group of Norwegians have been coming to Badminton for twenty years, and they and their wives seem to thoroughly enjoy the opportunity of being able to let their hair down away from any responsibilities of their home life. Sometimes they bring along a band for the post-shoot party. I, of course, feel bound to exhibit my skills in this department and join the musicians on stage, a service that I suspect is not offered by any other shoots in the land.

It is a tradition in Norway that, during a meal, speeches are made at regular intervals by the diners. When hosting the Norwegians in later life, my father, who was by now pretty deaf and at the best of times fairly impatient, muttered complaints at a louder volume than he was perhaps aware, along the lines of, 'I can't take much more of this,' or, 'Do get on with it.' Perhaps an unwise way to treat important clients, but I got the impression that the revellers just took this in their stride as part and parcel of what was on offer at Badminton.

The Crown Prince of Bahrain has also brought shooting parties to stay at Badminton. Prince Salman is a charming and cultured man and I have always enjoyed hearing him explain some of the complexities of his part of the world, but we also share a love of rock music, and on one occasion he brought along Eric Clapton as one of his guests.

Eric has been through some well-documented dark moments, but is the first to admit that nowadays he is inclined to transfer his addictive nature into other areas, and this has sometimes included shooting. I always look forward to talking to him not only about his rock past but also about more mundane matters; he has a splendidly down-to-earth way of explaining things, punctuated by an understated humour.

My father was one of two people I have known who was totally tone deaf (Tim Hanbury is the only other), so it was quite surprising that he really bonded with Eric. They seemed to thoroughly enjoy each other's company and he accepted Eric's invitation to attend one of his concerts at the Albert Hall. I don't think he was a musical convert, but he was rather fascinated to see the whole process at work and to observe a true master exercising his craft.

I had met Steve Winwood in New York when I was in my

thirties. Steve, a multi-instrumentalist, has over the years been in bands with Eric and was one of the biggest-selling artists in the States in the 1980s. As one listens to either Eric or Steve speak, there is the sobering thought at the back of one's mind that even if discussing something completely ordinary, you are actually talking to someone blessed with the ability to make their respective instruments speak in a way seldom achieved by anyone in history.

On one occasion, both Steve and Eric were shooting at Badminton along with Steve's spirited wife, Genia, who comes from Nashville. Over dinner, she asked my father about the mackerel pâté we were eating, and he replied, rather proudly, that Eric (which, coincidentally, was the name of his chef) had made it. Genia immediately leapt up and hollered down the table: 'Hey Eric, I never knew you could make mackerel pâté.'

The normally unflappable Clapton, who over the years had experienced the wilder excesses of the life of rock and roll, responded with a look of total bewilderment.

As well as Eric and Steve, I have also shot alongside Roger Waters and Nick Mason of Pink Floyd, albeit independently of each other. I met Roger staying with William and Annabel Astor and he subsequently asked me to join him at some of the finest shoots in England, as well as playing golf on American trips. I was ever keen to hear first-hand tales of drug-fuelled excess, synonymous with the name Pink Floyd. However, they both said that, even in the early days when

197

they were creating wild musical concepts such as 'Careful with that Axe Eugenie', they did not actually indulge that heavily, apart of course from the legendary acid casualty Syd Barrett. In different ways both Roger and Nick nurture a dry wit: out shooting with Nick, I sometimes used to discuss my own musical career and he once replied sagely, 'The trouble is, Harry, you want to be me, and I want to be you.'

The shooting season at Badminton when my father was Duke was pretty much non-stop, with house parties every weekend up until Christmas. I enjoy shooting, I like the way it gets one out of the house in winter and is the building block around some great weekends, but I'm not obsessed to the same degree as others. One person who really does adore it, however, is my friend Dave Ker. He was a regular guest of both mine and my father's, and on one occasion my father had also asked the billionaire Sid Bass, then principal share-holder in Disney. My father was particularly keen to give Sid a good day's sport after a very profitable share tip, so he placed the guns accordingly. Unfortunately, it was one of those days when the birds just wouldn't fly exactly where intended, always seeming to go over Dave and rarely over Sid. Eventually, much to the delight of the other guns, as mild misfortune for Dave tended to be a source of universal pleasure, my father bellowed at the gamekeeper in exasperation, 'Swap Mr Bass and Mr Ker.' It was noticeable that Mr Bass was quicker at taking his new position than Mr Ker.

Dave was a great friend of the Hong Kong businessman Sir David Tang, and on one occasion we were both invited by him to shoot at Garrowby, renowned for possibly being the best and most exclusive shoot in England. Their friendship was slightly unusual, and Tang delighted in tormenting Dave, saying that he could shoot only on the first of the two days that we were there, as there were too many guns. Dave said he was confident that Tang would relent, but as far as I could see he was totally determined to make his friend sit out a day of fun.

One of the other guests was Prince Michael of Kent, and in the final drive on the first day we were all shocked to see him firing his gun only to fall over backwards, obviously in considerable pain. We gathered around and it became obvious that he had damaged his shoulder quite badly, some mooting the idea of calling an ambulance. At that point I heard Dave's voice quietly in my ear: 'I think you'll find I'll be shooting tomorrow after all, Harry.'

For shooting purists, grouse are the preferred sport, but here I am a heretic. It is wonderful to be on top of a moor, but grouse shooting takes place in summer rather than winter, and a small voice in the back of my mind tells me that this is a good day's golf wasted. Also, by dint of the extra daylight, it goes on forever, so by the end of the day you are too exhausted to relish the evening festivities. I have given up grouse, therefore; a decision that some people find extraordinary.

Once, when I was shooting grouse in Northumberland, there was a sudden and unexpected cloudburst, and I found to my horror that the coat I had brought was not waterproof. After half an hour, I was soaked to the skin and couldn't have been wetter if I had jumped into a swimming pool, so I reluctantly insisted on going home.

The extraordinary thing is that even now, years later, I find myself accosted by people commenting, 'You're the chap who walked off the grouse moor after a rain shower,' rather in the manner of someone questioning an adult Oliver Twist as to why he had asked for more in the poorhouse. If I had walked off the golf course under similar circumstances, no one would have thought anything of it, but grouse shooting is anointed with an unassailable divinity by some of its more extreme adherents.

While shooting gets people out into the fresh air, it would be a mistake to think that driven pheasant shooting is in any way a healthy sport. The principal culprits are the many meals not normally on the agenda: a large, cooked breakfast, soup and sausages for elevenses, and even a totally unnecessary sandwiches-and-cake tea, reminiscent of my Eton days. Everything is washed down with alcohol, and by the end of the day one has sampled most of the offerings of a standard drinks tray. The only actual exercise undertaken is the short walk from Land Rover to one's peg, but somehow the bracing cold air builds up abnormal appetites. Quite often one feels liverish and exhausted prior to dinner and the only way to maintain form is to consume several sharpeners and crank the body back into action.

Not surprisingly, there is an element of tax to pay for this over-indulgence, and by the end of every shooting season I reliably find that I have put on at least half a stone. A lot of people nowadays consider the option of dry January, but for shooting folk dry February is more appropriate, although personally I prefer any dieting regime to be slightly less drastic.

At the end of one shooting season, I went along to the doctor concerning a routine renewal of a life insurance policy that was important in terms of inheritance tax planning for Badminton and was alarmed to be told a few days later that I had been turned down. I could not think of any aspect of my health that might have caused this. Due to the hypochondria instilled in me by Nanny Nelson, I even wondered, despite not being a member of any high-risk category, if I might have contracted AIDS.

It was something of a relief when I was told that the problem was that my liver function test had produced very poor readings, and that this was a common drip-drip effect of just generally drinking too much. Being a terrible hypochondriac, I decided to take some rather extreme action and gave up all alcohol for the best part of six months, and after this period my readings returned to normal. The whole thing had been a cautionary experience and it was good to know that I was capable of giving up without too much discomfort. I subsequently returned to the drinking fray, but reduced my overall consumption, including hardly ever drinking whisky, which up until then had been a default tipple.

Apart from shooting, my other principal hobby for the winter months has always been following National Hunt racing. This doesn't necessarily involve attending race meetings; mostly avidly recording and watching races of importance on television and taking detailed notes. This rather nerdish behaviour does have a purpose, as all roads lead to four magical days in March at the Cheltenham Festival, which I have never missed for the last thirty years.

The crowd at Cheltenham encompasses all areas of the social spectrum, brought together by a shared love of racing. The camaraderie is at its zenith in the Guinness village, where a huge throng gather from the moment the gates open, often in fairly adverse weather conditions, and some specialist drinkers manage to extend their pint quotient into double figures. It is not just a massive booze-up: the glue that cements the whole thing together is the horses themselves, and emotions can be very intense as these magnificent warriors strive for victory, sometimes displaying greatness and sometimes simple courage.

For many years my preferred lunch venue was the box owned by the Vestey family, where there was the perfect buffet, comprising homemade sandwiches and various other cold delicacies. Rather like the greedy ghost in the film

Ghostbusters, I would swarm across the table devouring everything in my path. It was then out on to the balcony to watch the sport, and to be engulfed in the famous Cheltenham roar as the first race set off.

I often used to stay for the races with Tony Lambton's daughter Rose and her partner Rhydian Morgan-Jones, who lived quite near Cheltenham. They tended to have an eclectic guest list, which sometimes included Rolling Stone Ronnie Wood and his wife Jo. Ronnie is now totally clean, but at this time he was still prone to casually tapping lines of cocaine on to the mantlepiece mid-conversation, until one year this prompted his twenty-year-old son to complain despairingly, 'Dad, please! Not in the living room.'

Ronnie seemed to have the constitution of an ox, but his forty-a-day cigarette habit, combined with substantial quantities of vodka, meant that having to leave for the races quite soon after breakfast was not part of his natural timetable. On one occasion I was deputised to go up to his room and see if he was ready. I knocked rather gingerly on the door and initially there was no answer, but eventually I heard Jo shaking him awake as she repeated in a mildly desperate crescendo, 'Ronnie ... Ronnie ... Ronnie.' It was quite a long time before there was any response at all, but gradually, from the depths of his chest, a terrible coughing bout began to emerge, and I knew he was alive. Remarkably, quite soon afterwards he was downstairs, dressed for racing and charming everyone with his cheeky persona.

Ronnie's charm lay partly in his enthusiasm for whatever he was doing. He once described the house he had just bought in Kingston. He was obviously pleased with the purchase but couldn't quite find the words to explain why. Suddenly it came to him. It was, he said, 'like a health farm', and it was rather touching that this represented his ideal of domesticity.

On one occasion I was at a party in London when Ronnie walked in and spied his friend, and former bandmate from the Faces, Rod Stewart. He seemed rather excited to see Rod and rushed up shouting greetings that perhaps didn't make total sense. Rod briefly tried to understand these outpourings but then, ever the showman, turned round with outstretched arms to the assembled crowd and shouted with great affection, 'Bollocks!'

In recent times I have entertained Cheltenham guests at Badminton, and one person who never missed joining us up until her death a few years ago was Lucy Ferry. Lucy had a sort of smouldering look about her, without being a conventional beauty, and cut a splendidly elegant figure at the races. She was born in Ireland and had a childhood based around hunting and racing, but, when she came to London, she found her inner rock chick, married Bryan Ferry and became a fashion icon. She was blessed with a wonderful sense of humour, and it was a true pleasure to trigger either a burst of her surprisingly deep laugh, or on occasion to see her sitting in a chair highly amused but choosing the option of silent hysterics.

CHAPTER 10

Duchess of Beaufort

My mother Caroline Beaufort in the library at Badminton,
where her spaniel Toby savaged a burglar.

WHILE THERE HAVE only been three men with the title Duke of Beaufort in the last hundred years, there have been five Duchesses. Three of them are alive today: my father's second wife, who he married in 2000, is Miranda, Duchess of Beaufort; my ex-wife of thirty years and the mother of my children is Tracy, Duchess of Beaufort, although she mostly goes by the name Tracy Worcester; and my wife Georgia is the current Duchess of Beaufort.

The track record of marriage in my family has not been straightforward, blending in with the colourful reality of many aristocratic marriages, past and present. Most celebrated, perhaps, was Master and Mary's marriage thanks to Master's zeal for women. Some of his girlfriends were married and he had to keep their husbands happy with the arrangement, a feat often achieved by asking them to come shooting at Badminton. He would stand laughing and flirting with the wife while using a varied armoury of distractions to keep the husband busy.

Gloria Cottesloe was not only Master's girlfriend but also the ghost writer of his autobiography, which famously he neither wrote nor read. I was once present at a shoot where we were told that her husband, Lord Cottesloe, should be given the best position in the line-up on every drive while the rest of us were subjected to a complicated numbering system to move us into a new place after each drive. Chaos ensued and Master, who wished to show the greatest courtesy to Lord Cottesloe on the shoot, if not in other areas, was furious with me for my inability to navigate this unworkable system.

Master's cunning was not always so successful. One day his chauffeur was driving him and Lady Cottesloe to the Great West Show in his very recognisable Bentley, with the personalised number plate of MFH 1. With some time to spare, Master instructed him to stop the car as he wanted Lady Cottesloe to enjoy the beautiful summer weather and to go for a short 'walk' together. When they returned, he instructed the chauffeur to resume the journey. Unfortunately, as they rounded the first corner a tractor stood blocking the road and no amount of hooting the horn could persuade the occupant to move on. Eventually the chauffeur got out and approached the farmer, but was quite surprised by his response: 'You can tell that dirty bugger that I know exactly what he's been doing and I ain't movin' until he gives me a fiver.' There was no choice but to pay the requisite sum.

The only girlfriend who really threatened his own marriage was the Duchess of Norfolk. Lavinia Norfolk was the wife of Bernard, 16th Duke of Norfolk, whose family are the prime lay Roman Catholics in Britain and whose ancestors have lived at Arundel Castle since the twelfth century. She was not a Catholic herself, which possibly made her less perturbed by any moral code her marriage might impose. Her affair with Master resulted in Mary moving out of Badminton for a short time and there was much talk of scandal. However, Mary was very popular with all the farm tenants, and they combined to say they would not allow the hunt on their land unless Master welcomed her back, and this nuclear threat caused a swift termination of the affair.

Many years later, Master came to dinner at my parents' house in the village and, by way of making conversation, my mother asked him who he thought was the greatest man of the twentieth century. He pondered for a few moments, and we fully expected him to suggest Winston Churchill or some such figure, but were both surprised when he said, 'Bernard Norfolk, for his splendid work as chairman of the Marylebone Cricket Club.'

Master and Mary's marriage was by no means unique. My mother's parents, Henry and Daphne, the sixth Marquess and Marchioness of Bath, had relished their part among the 'bright young things' set, who danced through the 1920s in fairly outrageous style, following the grim times of the First World War. Daphne chronicled these years in her autobiography *Mercury Presides*, written in her fifties, never having set pen to paper seriously before. When her friend Evelyn Waugh was asked what he thought of it, he was highly complimentary, but added that Daphne never mentioned any of her affairs, which he felt was rather like Field Marshal Montgomery writing his life story and not mentioning he joined the army.

This was much the same experience as my parents, who were only twenty-two when they married, very young by today's standards, but the moral climate was different in those days. A girl's reputation would be damaged by indulging in sex before marriage, while in many ways affairs within marriage were more acceptable than they are now. I think it is fair to say that my father never had any intention of adhering to the rules of fidelity. This made for recurring disappointments for my mother, who faced them stoically, telling me later, 'You either marry a man or a mouse.' Certainly, among their group of friends such behaviour was not out of the ordinary.

Tracy's mother Claire Ward moved to Italy to live with Tony Lambton after her divorce, although he never married her. Tony had been a defence minister in the Heath government but had to resign from parliament after his involvement with a prostitute was splashed in a classic *News of the World* exposé. He had had a very open marriage with his wife Bindy, so this was not a disaster in marital terms, and when asked on television by the political inquisitor Robin Day what he thought his constituents would think of such behaviour, he replied in his simultaneously mumbling and clear-cut high-pitched voice, 'I think they would say "lucky dog".'

Tracy's father, Claire's ex-husband, Peter Ward, probably had similar attitudes to love and marriage. He was an amiable father-in-law with a deceptively good business brain, but, while not an alcoholic, he certainly enjoyed maximising intake on a Saturday night. He would begin a story with something like, 'I was once in a brothel in Thailand . . .', before slumping back into his armchair, leaving his audience tantalised as to where this promising opening might have led.

Clare and Tony were living together at the time Tracy and I met. As it happened, Tony and Bindy were great friends of my parents, and Tony and my father had over the years shared a number of the same girlfriends. Tony was a glamorous but slightly sinister figure, always wearing dark glasses, and obsessed with all aspects of women and sex. He was also incredibly funny, and there was no greater pleasure than a long lunch in the garden talking and laughing with him.

His unusual descriptions were often uncannily accurate: a rather strange-looking girl 'had a face like a pointer. I keep expecting her to put up a covey of grouse,' he'd remark. Others resembled 'a ham', 'an axe', 'a fairground coconut that you throw balls at', 'a porcine brute with great underwater antelope nostrils' and 'a head like a half-eaten lollipop'.

He had a roster of girls and indulged in extensive telephone relationships with them all, discussing every aspect
of their lives, the more personal the better. Clare had incredible powers of self-delusion and spoke in flowery tones of
how much they loved each other. One night at Cetinale they
were overheard in the garden, where Clare had insisted on
taking Tony for a late-night walk. She said, almost swoon-
ing, 'Oh Tony, isn't it beautiful on a clear summer's night
under the stars?' Determined not to bow to this romantic
concept, he replied with a sort of mad clarity, 'I don't mind
the stars, but I can't stand that ghastly moon.' Tony was also
prone to disappearing for days on end for trysts with various lovers, causing Clare to lament how hard it was for him
having to constantly go off and meet financial advisers.

Between them they had created a remarkable garden at
Cetinale, and for his birthday Clare added an ornamental
pond, saying that he would enjoy sitting there in the evening watching the animals come down from the surrounding
hills to drink. Tony was less enamoured than she hoped by
this idea and said to me, 'Can you imagine anything more
boring than watching a load of animals drink water?'

My own mother dealt with my father's affairs and the
harder parts of her marriage by finding her own purpose in
life. She offered her services to numerous charitable causes,
where she became much loved for her eccentricity, which in
itself created great opportunities on the fundraising circuit.
These included stunts such as abseiling down a building,

where she somehow got stuck upside down, and accompanying other prominent charity mums to see the male strippers, the Chippendales. Afterwards she told me of her surprise to witness the hooting and hollering mode these rather genteel ladies got into when the men were on stage.

Her eccentricity was matched and overtaken by her friends in similar marriage set-ups. Bindy Lambton, for example, was infamous for her quirks. Tracy and I were asked to shooting weekends at Tony's Durham estate, Biddick. Tracy's mother Clare was not in attendance on these occasions. Instead, Bindy hosted, and although she and Tony barely spoke to each other, she was just as funny as him. Bindy enjoyed the act of laughter and was prepared to go to almost any lengths to generate this in herself, even if on occasion this required her to be fairly rude to other people to achieve the goal.

The family solicitor provided the perfect scapegoat: he was in the awkward position of being both guest and employee, and so had to absorb whatever was thrown at him. Once, by way of making conversation, Bindy asked him what sort of animal he would like to be. The solicitor thought for a little bit and then replied breezily, 'Oh I don't know Bindy, I think I'd like to be an eagle swooping around in the sky,' to which she came back as quick as a flash, 'More like a seagull with a face like yours.' He could not help registering considerable shock from this unprovoked attack, but any reaction was drowned by roars of laughter from Bindy.

She also liked to invent fantasies to satisfy this craving for laughter. One weekend Bindy's son Ned asked two very beautiful girls to stay, and she decided he had brought them along for the unlikely purpose of providing sexual gratification to the banker Sir Chips Keswick, who was one of the shooting guests. This would have been fine had she kept the joke to herself, but every time Chips went anywhere near the girls she shouted across the room, 'In you go Chips,' an instruction he obviously had no understanding of, and to which he could only blink in bewilderment every time it was issued.

In fact, Bindy was blithely unembarrassed about causing any collateral damage in pursuit of laughter. Her London house was blessed with a charming garden where she used to give lunches, but inevitably on occasion some food was left over. Rather than leave the task of taking it back into the house to her maid, she adopted the simpler policy of chucking it over the wall into her neighbour's garden. Somewhat predictably the neighbour made a formal complaint, but, undeterred, during subsequent lunch parties Bindy would become like a coiled spring, eventually finding it impossible to resist temptation and lobbing over any wastage before collapsing into laughter.

Inevitably, she sometimes went too far, and at a lunch at Badminton she clearly offended Princess Michael of Kent by commenting loudly on the size of her hands. My father was meant to be hosting this lunch but had to go out at the last minute, so my mother flung Johnson and me into the breach to entertain Princess Michael and an Italian woman she had brought along, who spoke very little English. I think I handled myself adequately, but when Johnson took over I was slightly alarmed to hear him launching into a story that was doing the rounds at the time about the actor Richard Gere and a lewd act involving a hamster. Luckily, Princess Michael whooped with delight, to such an extent that the Italian woman wanted to know the ins and outs of the joke. Princess Michael duly obliged and explained it in Italian. The woman's eyes slowly widened in horror, and she started fanning herself with her napkin in a state of shock, repeating, 'Ooh la la, ooh la la . . .', as if she were about to faint.

People embraced Bindy's eccentricity, especially Jools Holland, who adored her, deciding she should become a non-playing mascot for his band, rather like Bez from the Happy Mondays. She was wheeled on to the stage during the band's concerts and sat there amid a cacophony of noise, prompting the audience to question who this mysterious figure was, but Bindy was just happy to enjoy the experience in blissed-out euphoria. When she died a short time afterwards in 2003, Jools played the piano at her funeral.

Sadly, my own mother died several years before many of her friends, in 1995, aged only sixty-six. I was sitting in the garden at Badminton when she announced she had totally lost her appetite and didn't feel well. Determined that she had damaged her liver from excessive alcohol intake over the years, neither she nor any anyone else mentioned the dreaded C word. She was reluctant to go to the doctor, even when she suffered from jaundice, the liver damage narrative still seeming to make sense, but soon after this concerning development, she was diagnosed with cancer and was told she probably had no more than six months to live. This was obviously a great shock, but in reaction to the news she said, 'What a bugger,' declaring cancer to be a 'bloody bore' and telling her friends, 'If I thought it would do any good I would scream like a stuck pig, but instead I will have to carry on as normal.'

She remained in excellent spirits. A tube of some kind was inserted into her liver, which temporarily cured the jaundice, and she kept herself busy in typical style, by making lists about the advantages of having cancer, the first entry being 'Lose weight'. Ominously, I received a call from the doctor asking me to 'Keep an eye on your dad,' as he had been hit quite hard by the whole thing.

My mother's ill health brought my parents closer together. That Christmas I witnessed the rare sight of my father holding her hand at the dining room table. Nobody could say they had had a perfect marriage, but her illness had somehow made him realise how fond he was of her deep inside. In the last months of her life, I think it is fair to say that a sort of love affair developed between them, which was a great comfort to her. This included my father taking her to

Barbados for a winter break; the travelling was a real struggle for her, but I think she found it worthwhile for all the attention lavished upon her. On their return they made a day trip to London just to have a final look at Eaton Terrace, where they had spent much of their married life.

There were a string of poignant moments, starting with the annual Christmas party we throw for everyone who works for us. My mother had always insisted on walking along the tables to where the brass band was playing to congratulate them, waving her arms about and conducting the music in a rather haphazard way. There was something very moving in the fact that everyone in the room knew this was the last time they would see her performance, and I must admit that when I lay in bed that night tears flowed down my cheeks. She also insisted on coming out on the tenant farmers' shoot, where she was very touched to be presented with a huge bunch of flowers.

A lot of friends came to lunch to say their goodbyes. My mother always managed to be on top form for these visits, perhaps aided by the medicinal qualities of the odd whisky. One of the visitors was her brother Alexander Bath, who she had not been close to for a long time, after he had over-reacted to some perceived insult from my father. Alexander had become incensed that my father, a pilot himself, had been slightly mocking about his microlight plane and vowed never to enter the house again. When he knew my mother was dying, however, he returned to Badminton with one of his wifelets, who had the manner of a suburban secretary. Conversation at lunch proved awkwardly stilted, but after the meal everyone relaxed, and my mother and Alexander reverted to a sort of baby talk shared in their nursery sixty years earlier, and they were roaring with laughter by the time he made his departure. The silliness continued in his thank-you letter, when he reported that he had been asked by a historian for the best words to use when describing genitalia. He had originally suggested 'cock', 'cunt' and, slightly obtusely, 'fuck', but was now having social anxiety about the whole thing and asked his older sister if perhaps he should have just said 'old man'.

Representatives of the seventy-six charities of which my mother was a patron organised a presentation of an honorary doctorate to her, for which she wore full university regalia. There is a picture of her sitting in these clothes with what she described at the time as 'a rather silly smile of contentment' on her face. I accompanied my mother when she gave her final guided tour of the house. Over the years she had developed a rather brilliant commentary combining historical knowledge with elements of gossip about the sexual proclivities of our ancestors. It was during this last appearance that I realised how frail she had become. She began enthusiastically but after about three rooms she suddenly became exhausted and had to sit down.

After this her decline sped up. She still had periods of clarity and there was rather a touching moment when my daughter Bella, who was two, insisted that my mother go out into the garden and see a ladybird she had found. The whole scene was somehow reminiscent of the film *The Godfather* when Marlon Brando is playing with his grandson in the garden shortly before he dies. On another occasion she was watching Monster's daughter Ella playing on the carpet and she said rather philosophically how extraordinary it was that two years ago she had not existed, the unspoken message being that shortly she herself would be disappearing into a similar state of nothingness. Despite this she was still keen on discussing her funeral and gave me the responsibility of ensuring that the format more resembled an Irish wake than anything mournful.

Eventually the time came when there was no alternative but for her to retire to bed, and it was fairly obvious there wasn't long to go. The doctors upped the painkiller dose and, from then on, she wasn't that coherent, but the last conversation I had with her began with a request for whisky, and when I discussed how strong it should be I was reprimanded by the words, 'Don't be silly.' I then stood about not really knowing what to say, and she suddenly indicated that I should bend closer to her and whispered, 'I love you.' It was somehow a great relief for me to answer back that I loved her too.

From that moment on she was basically asleep and was expected to die soon, but in fact she confounded predictions by holding on for nearly two weeks. She was not really aware of what was going on, but the nurse suggested we keep talking to her as she could still hear us, so I went up and said, 'Mum, it's Bunter,' and was quite surprised by her mumbled response, before she drifted back into sleep, of 'Bunter the nit,' an affectionate nickname Monster had given me when we were children. The doctor was really quite surprised that she was still alive, confiding that he had given her enough heroin to kill a horse, but that might be explained by the fact that her liver had taken such a battering from alcohol over the years that it had no difficulty in fending off this latest attack.

My mother finally died on 22 April 1995. I was present at the time, but it was not really an event as such in that she seemed to just drift from life into death. The flag above the house was lowered to half-mast, but, despite the sadness, the main sensation was one of relief that medication had stopped her last days being excessively painful. There was, though, a tangible emptiness in the parts of the house that she had made her own.

The obituaries were very complimentary, detailing both her good works and her general character as well as hints of her eccentricity. Monster and I both read at her funeral, touched by how people of all ages and backgrounds had taken the trouble to come. The numbers were such that we had to arrange for an overspill into the orangery at Badminton. My mother would have been amused by one consequence of the overspill provisions. Over several years she had developed a rather irritating habit of refusing to answer the telephone, even if she was sitting beside it. The reason for this was that she used to receive occasional calls from a man called Robert de Stackpole, asking if they could meet up in some way. By all accounts the man was harmless enough, but a terrible bore, and she was desperate to avoid having to go through the stressful procedure of creating excuses not to see him. This was very tiresome for the rest of us though, if, for example, we were lying in the bath when the phone rang, and we knew that she was within six inches of it but exerting an iron determination not to pick up.

Obviously, everyone wanted to be in the church for the service, but the ushers had a detailed seating plan, and nobody complained except for one person. That of course was Robert de Stackpole, who caused a terrible commotion and tried to barge his way in, showing equal determination about contacting my mother in death as in life, and I'm sure she would have appreciated the way her gatekeepers ejected him.

She would have also enjoyed when Master's old girl-friend Peggy De L'Isle was standing among the guests after the service drinking tea, when suddenly there was a very audible twang. The room was briefly silenced but, as conversation slowly picked up again, I noticed Peggy lift-ing her feet in a rather dignified way and then walking away. It turned out the elastic on her rather large bloomers had snapped, causing them to fall to the floor, and she had sensibly elected just to step out of them unobtrusively and leave them there.

As per my mother's wishes, her funeral was more of a celebration of life than anything sad, but it was not as eccentric as it might have been. When her own father, Henry Bath, had died in the 1990s, he lived up to his reputation for eccentricity by leaving specific instructions that he was to be buried in an orange shirt, and that his coffin should be driven as fast as possible to the church without endangering life.

*

When it came to my own marriage with Tracy, it started off well. It was a slight relief that our first child was a son, as he secured the succession. Both of my parents were delighted, my mother instructing the vicar to ring out the church bells and my father presenting Tracy with a top-of-the-range camera. I also received lots of congratulatory calls.

Tracy was a very modern mother, feeling no embarrassment breastfeeding in public. I think this slightly unsettled both of my parents, who remained polite about it, though Sunny Marlborough was less discreet. Witnessing the operation being conducted in the library at Badminton, he was provoked to comment, 'The milk bar's open chaps,' followed by the traditional Churchillian snort.

By the time our third child was born, we were based between The Cottage and London, but our relationship became increasingly distant. Leading ever more separate lives over the span of thirty years worked to a point. But in some ways our marriage mirrored the set-up of my own parents, who spent time apart for much of their lives.

Tracy has always been a loving mother to our children and a pioneer in the environmental world, campaigning passionately for things that have now become part of mainstream thinking. With hindsight though, I would say that we were never particularly well suited. Our marriage had the pretence of being functional in that we shared a lot of the same friends and enjoyed doing things with the children, but when it came down to quietly enjoying each other's company there was little common ground. I dare say we would have grown apart anyway, but it was certainly exacerbated by her total passion for the environment that became her main priority in life.

For many years I actively searched for space from my marriage, socialising in London to distance myself from Tracy. During the 1990s, Johnson and I used to spend a lot of time with an Iranian called Shahriar Bakhtiar. Johnson's marriage had broken up, so Shahriar, who always seemed to be accompanied by lots of beautiful girls and adored nightclub hedonism, was the perfect accomplice in the quest for pleasure. Dinners were usually in the legendary restaurant San Lorenzo, where we always had the same table at the bottom of the stairs, from where we could survey the glitterati arriving.

Shahriar had been sent to boarding school in England, and was used to dividing his time between Iran and London, but when in 1979 the Islamic Revolution took hold in his homeland he escaped on the same plane as the Shah of Iran's wife, never to return. As one of the rich elite he no longer had anything in common with the new regime and I sometimes reflected on how strange it must have been for him not to feel any allegiance to the country in which he had been born.

Shahriar's family brought plenty of money with them and his extravagance was legendary. Sometimes he would take over entire top floors of hotels for three-day parties. By the time I got to know him in the late 1980s his fortune was already starting to diminish, and this slowly continued until his death in 2020, by which time he was left with virtually nothing. Despite this, he always maintained complete dignity, and this was appreciated by the Goldsmiths, who looked after his basic needs and liked having him around almost as a member of the family.

Our mutual friend Taki was also very fond of him, and I remember one evening in San Lorenzo when, in particularly vociferous form, Taki stood up and pointed at Shahriar, shouting, '*Why* do we like him? He never speaks, he never laughs, he knows nothing of politics,' before being ordered to sit down by the long-suffering proprietor, Myra. We all roared with laughter but there was no denying there was an element of truth to all this, the key fact being that there was something about Shahriar's presence that was a positive, even if it was not obviously on show. Robin Birley, a half-brother of the Goldsmith boys, went even further, saying that even if Shahriar were an arms dealer he would still adore him, and there was no doubt that he did inspire a mysterious devotion. I still miss his regular plaintive cry, 'For God's sake Bunter, where are the girls?'

My time spent in London made for an unconventional marriage. We possibly could have continued with this arrangement indefinitely, but I began to find it increasingly difficult when Tracy's passions for environmental causes impinged on every aspect of our lives. I found myself becoming bored, and the fact I didn't share such a key part of her life's focus separated us further. One of Tracy's main objections to life with me was that there was not enough 'intellectual' conversation. The problem was that we both had different definitions of what that word meant; I enjoy nothing more than a serious discussion about British politics, for example, but she would always try to refocus the topic to environmentalism, which I found narrow-minded. In the end, our differences became intolerable to me, and no doubt to her.

The other disappointment about this situation was that Tracy's relationship with my father completely broke down; he had even less patience concerning her subject than I did, and once described her as being 'a good woman, but impossible to be in the room with for more than five minutes'. He was very irritated by the stream of interviews she gave to the newspapers, purportedly to promote her cause, but in fact coming over as criticisms of the Badminton estate and the way it was run. This in turn led to Tracy not wanting to accompany me on my regular visits for meals at Badminton, which wouldn't have mattered in itself, but meant that the children stayed behind with her, and therefore never achieved the special relationship with my father that he enjoyed with his other grandchildren.

I dare say the marriage would have ended earlier if we both had not had independent lives to fall back on. Tracy and I came from fairly liberal backgrounds. She had as a principal thesis of her life, perhaps because of the pain of her own parents' divorce, that it was a duty to have marital flexibility, to keep the show on the road for the sake of the children. In fact, she was prone to lecturing friends who had run into similar difficulties about these responsibilities, causing one to complain, 'Tracy, I'm not a rainforest.' What this meant in practice was that, from the mid-1990s on, I had a number of affairs, which lent some excitement to life as well as, in some cases, creating lifelong friendships.

I had assumed that things would jog on indefinitely in this way, but the truth was that our marriage was now a sort of slow grind, giving limited pleasure to either of us. I found myself spending more time in London or going to stay with friends for the weekend on my own, and thoughts of how life would be if we got divorced crossed my mind with increasing regularity. I was concerned, though, about the effect this might have on my relationship with the children, and by the financial and housing implications of a divorce.

Actually to take the plunge would need a more powerful catalyst. And that arrived when I became completely smitten with someone who became very special to me. Prior to this, I had rather subscribed to the Prince Charles 'whatever love means' school of thought with regard to relationships, but, not far short of my sixtieth birthday, I absolutely did understand what it meant for the first time. To start with we were just friends, but after her divorce our friendship magically evolved into an affair. Every time I drove over the Chiswick flyover into London my heart soared at the prospect of seeing her, and she was constantly on my mind even when we were not together. But the relationship itself was something of a rollercoaster. Truly wonderful times were interspersed with the trauma of breaking up and then somehow being drawn back together again. I suppose in my heart of hearts I sensed that this could not be sustained over the long term, but I felt that life is too short not to take these chances. I decided that whatever the outcome, Tracy and I should get divorced. When the affair finally did end, I could only reflect that it had been a totally life-enhancing experience and felt that from a rather late starting point I was finally beginning to grow up.

I am grateful to Tracy for not hiring some hotshot lawyer and trying to take me for all I'd got, but, even when conducted on a relatively amicable basis, divorce is a stressful business, and I dread to think what it is like for couples who genuinely can't stand the sight of each other. The main point of contention for us was housing. I assumed that if I gave her the house in London and one of the nicer houses on the estate, while staying in The Cottage myself, that would be deemed fair. I was advised, however, as it was likely that in the not-too-distant future I would be moving into Badminton House, that a judge might decree I should move out of The Cottage until then. After being given that advice, I returned home that evening and opened the front door feeling an overwhelming sense of sadness about losing the house in which, one way and another, I had lived for much of my life. As it turned out, Tracy agreed to have another house in the village, provided it was guaranteed that she could return to The Cottage when I moved out.

During the divorce, I first set eyes on Georgia Powell, who was going through the same process. When we finally got together a couple of years later, I was still a bit scarred by the trauma of the ups and downs of my love life, and it was initially something of a slow-burn. As time went on, however, I came to the wonderful realisation that it is possible to enjoy 'une grande passion' without constantly worrying that it might crash to an end at any moment. I feel lucky at my relatively advanced age to have landed so spectacularly on my feet with someone with whom I feel totally comfortable and whose attitude to life is similarly all-embracing. In addition, Georgia accepts most of my imperfections, gets on with my friends and shares my enjoyment of meeting new people.

Georgia comes from a literary and artistic family. Her grandfather was the writer Anthony Powell, who wrote the twelve-volume series of novels *A Dance to the Music of Time*, and her family are all involved in the arts in some shape or form. I can't deny that she too has many talents. Having studied Classics at Oxford, she became a successful journalist and teacher. *Vogue* once likened her beauty to that of a 1930s heroine, but the quality I love most about her is her wonderful sense of humour. Her father, brother and sister-in-law are successful in the television world, and I like to joke that I have been welcomed into the family partly on the back of my extreme knowledge of the medium.

Georgia has two high-achieving children from her first marriage, who I have become very fond of. Harry has two useful skills in the modern age: he is an artist who designs video games, and also has an ability to relax that would be the envy of any stress therapist. His sister Hope got a high-profile job in journalism within days of leaving university, and I am confident that she will use her barbed but non-malicious wit to write a book at some stage. Her ability as a wordsmith popped out at an early stage of my relationship with Georgia; Hope observed me suffering a particularly bad hangover and commented that it was time I realised I was no longer 'such a young rapscallion', a description that

I only vaguely recognised from somewhere in the recesses of children's fiction.

Another pleasure of being with Georgia is that I have got to meet a whole group of new people and, as she is seventeen years younger than me, I had not met that many of them before. At Oxford, she had lived in an all-male household where academic achievement was not allowed to interfere totally with the wilder shores of hedonism. When she worked in television documentaries, the obituary department at the *Telegraph* and as a teacher, she built up a varied portfolio of friends. She also spent much of her childhood in Somerset, where she still has a house, and it was a pleasure for me to be introduced to her friends from that world.

These include Danny Goffey and Pearl Lowe, who are in some ways an unlikely couple, but it is one of those situations that works. They both have a musical background in that Danny is the drummer in Supergrass, while Pearl was also successful in the 1990s indie band Powder, before moving on to become an interiors and fashion designer. Danny is incredibly funny, one of those people where you never know exactly which way their humour is going to go, the only consistency being that he always has the air of a boy up to mischief as he makes the room laugh. Pearl has a dark beauty about her and looks on, perhaps more amused by these performances than she is prepared to admit. I think it is fair to say that she is the financial brains behind their operation, but I would back them both to survive most problems that life decides to throw their way.

We share mutual friends too, including the actress and great friend of Georgia's, Annabel Mullion, who introduced us, although I'm surprised that we had never met before, as so many of our friendships seemed intertwined. Don McCullin and his wife Catherine Fairweather are Somerset neighbours of Georgia who I knew before they got together. Don is probably the greatest war photographer of his generation and, even in his eighties, still cannot resist trips to ravaged war-torn lands such as Syria to ply his trade. He was a great friend of Mark Shand, Camilla Parker Bowles's brother, and retains a similar boyish joy to Mark in recounting his exploits. He adores nothing more than a bit of laddish chat but is something of an enigma. Once I was with him and Mark Shand, and Mark was laughingly telling the story of how they had been accosted by men with guns on one of their trips together. Don's face suddenly darkened, and he said in very sombre tones, 'I wasn't laughing. I have seen the look on men's faces when they are about to kill many times, and those people had real darkness in their eyes.'

Both of us also know Dominic West and his wife Catherine, who I have admired for many years. Georgia had met Dominic through Annabel and also through Polly Astor, who is the mother of Dominic's first child. Polly had come briefly into my life when Tracy had met her, inviting her for a weekend at The Cottage after she had recently separated from Dom.

I didn't meet Polly again until I was with Georgia, but her impish charm was always apparent, and it is rather fascinating in the scheme of things to think that her grandmother was the legendary MP Nancy Astor, and her first cousin is my friend William Astor, whose stepdaughter is Samantha Cameron. Furthermore, her father was Michael Astor, who used to stay at Badminton with my parents, and Polly has clear memories of playing at my mother's dressing table when she was a child.

It was through Polly that I met Emily Mortimer, who is one of her best friends. I remember this encounter, as Emily later told Georgia that she thought I was very good looking and, such is my vanity, I immediately adored her. Another person who admits to being easily flattered is Ollie Lane Fox, who always says that if somebody likes him he cannot resist liking them back. He was one of the men who shared a house with Georgia at Oxford and always displays such a professional charm that we have christened him Le Champion in reference to this skill. His wife, Hatty, has a face of almost angelic innocence, although this belies the wild tales of her youth when, even if she wasn't involved in the wildness herself, she seems to have been ever present as a benign observer.

Dominic and Catherine West rented a house on the Badminton estate for a few years before buying their own place nearby, and they remain regular visitors. Dominic is extremely funny and possibly slightly more sensitive than meets the eye. He certainly enjoys being an actor and the effect his skills can have on an audience, once sending my cook at The Cottage weak at the knees for about three weeks by thanking her, and adding, 'You've been watching that bedroom scene from *The Affair*, haven't you?' His talents are wide-ranging, and his portrayal of the serial killer Fred West certainly required him to channel an inner darkness. He has remarkable energy, often being the last to bed and the first to rise to take part in whatever outdoor activity is required of him the next day. Despite his fame he doesn't live the Hollywood lifestyle but doesn't mind dipping into it: he and Catherine will happily drive their children around in a camper van for the summer holidays, but occasionally find the time to drop in on the likes of George and Amal Clooney en route. Something of an action man, Dom accepted an invitation to walk to the South Pole with a group of adventurers including Prince Harry a few years ago. Ironically, he went on to play Prince Harry's father in *The Crown*. We holidayed together in Kenya just after he had filmed the scene sharing the news of Princess Diana's death to Princes William and Harry. He told us that he had originally played the scene very emotionally but after the publication of Prince Harry's autobiography *Spare*, which implied that Prince Charles had been unable to express his emotions, the scene had to be reshot.

A strange link is that another friend and neighbour, Julia Samuel, was one of the people who actually consoled the Princes after their mother's death. When I first knew Julia she was part of the London party scene of my youth, but she has now become a psychotherapist of considerable renown, specialising in bereavement counselling, and has written three bestselling books on the subject. She was a great friend of Princess Diana and used these skills to help the young Princes through the trauma of losing their mother. They are still in regular contact with her, and she is a godmother to Prince George. Georgia and I watched the 2017 election at the Samuels' house, and, with Corbyn's Labour coming within a whisper of winning, I was close to requiring grief counselling of my own.

The night before the 2019 election we went to a party in London, hosted by Anthony and Carole Bamford, and then two days afterwards we stayed at their house in Staffordshire for their shoot, and it was interesting to compare the feelings of anticipation at the former event and relief at the latter. Carole, who has always retained a hint of rock chick about her, is a consummate hostess, and staying at their house provides a model of perfection that everyone can aspire to. Anthony is quietly spoken with an excellent sense of humour, but I suspect he is a tougher businessman than this might imply, having inherited the multinational company JCB from his father and then taken it to far greater heights on his own watch.

Another friend of theirs is their Gloucestershire neighbour Jeremy Clarkson. He is rather what you would expect from his television persona, in that he delights in being outrageous and is really very funny indeed. One thing that should never be underestimated is his intelligence, which he uses to frame his sentences in a totally original way alongside his bombastic delivery. Recently, he has capitalised on all these talents with the television series *Clarkson's Farm*, in which he manages not only to be incredibly entertaining but also to inform his audience about the difficulties of farming in today's world, a subject I know something about myself but could never have made as interesting.

Although we do a lot of socialising, Georgia and I have always been very comfortable in each other's company. I am a bad traveller, and before flying anywhere I tend to sleep poorly, not because of a fear of flying but due to worry about the stress and aggravation of the whole process. Family holidays with my children tended to provoke embarrassing outbursts at airports. With Georgia, however, we seem to fall into a similar rhythm and the only outbursts are benign: childish hysterics as we sit together. In 2017, during a brief holiday to New York, as we settled into our hotel I found myself clumsily suggesting that we should get married, not least because it seemed the most natural thing in the world to do. Happily, she accepted.

CHAPTER 11

Becoming Duke

Presenting the prizes at the Beaufort Hunt point-to-point.

IN 2017, I became the 12th Duke of Beaufort. Out of the seventy-four dukedoms originally created, only twenty-two remain today. No dukes have been made since the Duke of Westminster in 1874, although the late Queen offered a dukedom to Winston Churchill, but only when it had been established that he was not going to accept it.

I am slightly ashamed to say that my knowledge of my family history is patchy at best. But I have always been aware of the pressure on me to keep the estate intact and I do see how astonishing it is to be able to trace so many generations of a single family back so far.

Maybe because of the original high stakes of being battle leaders or advisers to the Kings and Queens of England, there seem to be a number of unique and memorable characters with a certain liveliness in aristocratic families. This trait is possibly why many have been labelled with madness. My maternal uncle, Alexander Bath, was publicly known for his alternative lifestyle. He virtually never came to Badminton because he and my father didn't get on, and my mother was not particularly close to him either. All reports of Alexander are that as a young man he was among the best looking of his generation. His father, Henry Bath, was badly clobbered by inheritance tax when his own father had died young and was determined not to cause a similar problem. As a result, he handed over much of the Longleat estate to Alexander when he was about twenty-five. This was in spite of the fact that the father–son relationship was fractious; the need to keep the estate intact trumped all. In the 1960s Alexander grew his hair long, cultivated an almost biblical beard and started wearing extraordinary robes, a look he maintained for the rest of his life. He rarely changed these clothes or had a bath. Adopting some aspects of the free love movement, he announced very publicly that he had no interest in a conventional marriage but wanted rather to enjoy an endless stream of 'wifelets', to whom he was not formally married.

He did, however, want a son and heir to whom he could pass on Longleat and his title, so he married the Hungarian actress Anna Gaël, but with the mutual understanding that fidelity would not be part of their vows. He was probably rather disappointed when their first child, Lenka, was a girl. Not wanting to be disappointed again, he insisted on taking his wife's vaginal temperature at specific times of the month, often in very public places, Alexander having a theory that it was more likely a boy would be conceived under the right conditions. Whether or not the science of this was correct, it did prove successful, and their next child was a son, Ceawlin.

As a symbol of his priapic nature, Alexander began a life-long project of creating *Kama Sutra* murals, which he painted on entire walls at Longleat. They were very explicit, depicting naked characters in a multitude of sexual contortions, but perhaps not of the highest artistic merit. At the end of his life there was a major rift between him and his son Ceawlin, who removed them the moment ownership of the estate passed on to him.

At the other end of the eccentricity scale, there are characters such as Gerald Grosvenor, 6th Duke of Westminster. We both used to stay at Hever Castle in the 1970s, with our mutual friend Sarah Astor, daughter of Lord Astor of Hever. Gerald was a charming and rumbustious character who liked nothing more than a good scrap, so the very long corridors at Hever were the ideal location for him to charge mindlessly about. At the end of one such passage stood a full-length mirror, and it seemed only natural to Gerald, in full gallop, that in front of him appeared a willing participant coming towards him for a friendly fight. He was extremely surprised to crash into the glass at full speed, ending up spending the night in casualty.

Shortly afterwards, Gerald's father died, and on inheriting he became much more responsible. Taking on a legendary amount of charitable work, he dropped out of my life to adopt a more conventional rich aristocrat's existence. Years later I saw him at the wedding party of David and Samantha Cameron. I was a bit out of it, swaying gently to the pounding techno music, when he came up to me and said, 'Parties. Can't stand 'em. Can't wait to get back at the grouse . . . don't you agree?' In my slightly euphoric state, I couldn't land on a single area of agreement, and he drifted away slightly disappointed.

I like to think that my attitude to owning an estate, whilst responsible, is not as conventional as Gerald Westminster's, something that was ingrained in me by my father. He was always full of sound advice, although he was not one of nature's delegators – a factor that I'm sure affects many landed families, as estates seem to thrive on a certain hierarchy and inbuilt deference to the top man.

Although an estate like Badminton has obvious capital wealth, its income is comparatively small and management costs are huge, so selling land for development or redeveloping it oneself has always been one of the traditional ways that landlords like us have survived. My father had all sorts of ideas for schemes on the estate. He was always making proposals that had merit on aesthetic grounds, but his relations with the local planning authority were tricky and he began to feel that one particular planning officer was turning things down for political reasons.

My father invited this man to lunch to show him round the estate, hoping that his legendary charm would make him see sense. The man arrived. A caricature of a left-wing council worker, he wore sandals despite the fact that some muddy terrain would inevitably be involved in the tour. The meeting started inauspiciously when he announced that he would be unable to stay for lunch, for fear that it might be construed as taking some sort of bribe.

Undaunted, we set off on our tour and my father put on a very professional show, but it was obvious that it was being received with only modest appreciation. Eventually we arrived at a property that had a disused coach house in the garden, and my father explained expansively how he thought this could be converted into a special dwelling. But the planner suddenly interjected with the self-important disdain of a 1970s lecturer at a polytechnic: 'Excuse me, but under section four, paragraph three of the Town Planning Act, no windows can be added to any conversion within the curtilage of a listed building.'

My father had already taken a strong dislike to the man, and this was too much for him. Exploding at full volume, he exclaimed, 'For God's sake, how can a building not have windows?' The tour was a disaster and, with little point in continuing, the man left. Fortunately, nowadays we have adopted a more conventional approach to planning matters with considerably more success.

Money and finances were always the prime concern and so political changes were always keenly and often nervously observed by my father. When the 2008 recession hit, for us as a family, as for so many others, there seemed to be a genuine possibility that our lives would be irrevocably changed, and my father even began speculating about leaving Badminton and living in a house on the estate. He had just celebrated his eightieth birthday when the crash happened, but he was in remarkably good shape for a man of his age. He used to go to Barbados for a month every winter, where he befriended some of the rich Irish tycoons who followed a similar holiday pattern. One of them, on coming to shoot at Badminton, jokingly asked me if I could bottle up some of my father's DNA for him so that he could be similarly active when he reached that age. The reality was that my father was just beginning to feel his years. He suffered from various aches and pains and could no longer play golf to a standard that was enjoyable, and he was also experiencing occasional fainting episodes.

Increasingly aware of his mortality, as I had similarly been when my mother was ill, I was reminded of a scene from *The Godfather*, as he persistently took me aside and offered suggestions of what I should do when he died. I felt rather like Al Pacino replying to Marlon Brando, who is equally persistent in warning his son about who will eventually try to betray him. 'Yeah Pop,' says Pacino, 'you told me that already.' But hopefully my father found the whole procedure comforting.

In middle age I sometimes compared my own health to a satisfactory car that required a few more visits to the garage than before. The most serious of these was an operation I needed for an enlarged prostate, which was fairly unpleasant, as the emergency was triggered by my being unable to pee, despite desperately wanting to. I was also quite fortunate, as these symptoms could have indicated cancer. Thankfully, after the operation had been completed, the relevant equipment seemed to be in working order, which is not always the case in such situations. Such experiences get one thinking that life is short, and one should be careful not to waste it.

This idea of embracing life was inadvertently epitomised by my school friend George Kershaw. In 2015 I was at The Cottage and was slightly alarmed to see an air ambulance hovering above a field where hunting was in progress. I jokingly remarked that I hoped it wasn't for George Kershaw, who had a long-standing reputation for extreme bravery matched with moderate riding skills and had been lucky not to be fatally injured in a fall two years earlier. As news developed further, it became no laughing matter. The ambulance was indeed for Kershaw, and he was likely totally paralysed.

Up until that moment Kershaw had led an almost perfect life. When the bank he worked for was taken over he made a substantial amount of money and decided to wind down his connections with the City and spend more time indulging his passions of hunting and skiing. His love of these sports was based around a constant flirtation with danger and, on top of endless hunting accidents, while skiing he was also caught in an avalanche, which he was lucky to survive.

During this time, he also became a somewhat unlikely youth icon, aided by rather strange specialities for a man of his age, such as dancing on the mantlepiece. There was also a lot of love around and I remember his son Sam making a speech at his thirtieth birthday saying that his friends almost unanimously said that they could not think of better parents to have than George and Sarah. They certainly did seem to have something close to the perfect marriage.

After the accident Kershaw had to endure a long period of rehabilitation at Stoke Mandeville hospital. His sense of humour and positive attitude remained acutely intact. During visiting him in hospital another friend of his and I got into a discussion about having had prostate operations, whereupon Kershaw suddenly interjected, 'Well, aren't I the lucky one!' Above all, however, he was lucky to have Sarah, who dutifully drove down and saw him every single day, and it was uplifting to observe the strength of their love and mutual respect despite everything they've been through.

One of the cruelties of Kershaw's accident was that it physically limited his ability to laugh at full strength. Ever since our schooldays, this had been a pleasure we often indulged in together, one occasion ending in us both collapsed in hysterics for an absurd amount of time. Eventually we took breath, he blinked at me, looking rather surprised, and asked, 'What was I laughing at?', but then added as an afterthought, 'Oh yes, I remember,' which set off an even more cacophonous outburst. The original joke was again soon forgotten, but just as it had been at Eton, our pleasure derived from the act of laughter itself, rather than from any subtlety in the remark.

Kershaw has never let anything stop him from enjoying himself. His wheelchair is a well-known sight at parties, careering dangerously around the dance floor, and when the Kershaw family gave a party themselves, he had to be dissuaded on the grounds of taste from insisting on having 'the disabled' as the dress code. He even seriously considered taking up sky diving, but that project remains a work in progress.

During Kershaw's rehabilitation, my father's health continued to decline. Whenever the subject of George's accident came up, he repeated how he felt so sorry for him not having anything to look forward to, but he was also of course referring to his own predicament. The only good thing was that there was never going to be any question of his having to finish his life in hospital, as he was attended by an army of nurses, and his second wife, Miranda, who was devoted to him. Together with the staff in the house, they did a wonderful job of looking after him.

Many an heir to an estate such as ours has had problems with stepmothers, but Miranda has always had such a love of Badminton that she did everything in her power to create a smooth handover. She continues to live on the estate, and I count her as a very good friend.

When Georgia met my father, he was already on a downward trajectory, but he liked her very much and was cheered by her visits to the house, while she was still able to glimpse his old charm. I had always assumed that, as someone whose life had been blessed with good fortune, his death would be quick and untroubled, but it turned out to be a long, drawn-out process. During the last five years of his life, he suffered a number of small strokes that gradually immobilised him, first to a wheelchair and finally to bed. The saddest thing about his decline was that, as a very restless character, he had lived his whole life in fear of boredom, and now that was exactly what he had to endure.

I had regular meals with him and in a strange way grew closer to him, but his mood was very much up and down. Sometimes I achieved the mini triumph of making him laugh really quite heartily, but on other occasions there were real signs that he had lost his zest, and he was also prone to becoming muddled. Throughout the whole time, though, he maintained a dignity. One moving moment came at his final Horse Trials, where he watched the show-jumping from his Land Rover in the middle of the arena. When the hounds did their traditional display at the end of the competition, they were taken on a deliberate detour for him to see them, rather like young cadets being shown to an ageing general.

Perhaps the strangest thing for me and the rest of the

family was that someone who had been such a dominant figure in our lives was now diminishing before our eyes. He showed surprising resilience, and I can remember his doctor saying that they didn't think he would make Christmas, but then he survived until the following August. Eventually we were summoned home and gathered in his room like a scene in a Victorian novel. I found tears pouring down my cheeks watching him there on the cusp of life and death, although in fact he once again made a slight recovery.

As we awaited the end, I spent an afternoon playing golf on my own at Stinchcombe, which had been such a regular feature of life with my father, and the spiritual side of the game once again came to the fore as I played as well as I had done in a long while. Then, the next day, when I went to the funeral of our gamekeeper Mervyn, I received the message that my father had finally died. I returned to the house and went up to his bedroom, where he was lying on the bed as if asleep.

As I headed back to The Cottage, I saw Robbie, one of the butlers at Badminton, standing at the edge of the park, staring wistfully into the middle distance; then, going down the drive, I saw my brother Eddie also moping sadly around. I stopped the car to have a brief word with him. Eddie walked slowly over and stuck his head through the window, before surprising me by saying in a deep Gloucestershire accent, 'Evenin' Your Grace.' This little piece of gallows humour was both comforting and a reminder of the changing of the guard.

My father's funeral took place a week after he died. He was not a religious man so the service was short, but it included a number of readings from his grandchildren. Anyone who knew him was welcome and about one and a half thousand people came, which meant that a huge tent had to be erected by the house for both the overspill from the church, and the refreshments afterwards. The guests came from all walks of life and ages, and it was, above all, a celebration of the life of a popular and respected man. In the way that funerals often are, it felt like a welcome release from all the tension and sadness that had preceded it.

The next day Georgia and I dined with some friends of hers, Renshaw and Sarah Hiscox, who live in an old mill house quite near Badminton. I had never been there before and was unaware of the unusual stone staircase descending to the basement from their living room; within seconds of my arrival, I found myself flying through the air and cracking my head on the stone floor below. Luckily, despite a cartoon-sized bruise on my head, I was only mildly dazed, but if I had fallen differently, it could have been more serious; somebody commented that it could have marked the shortest ascendancy to a dukedom in English history.

We moved into Badminton eight months after my father's death, having installed a consignment of six televisions that were placed in any room where it might take our fancy to watch the great device. It was testament to the popularity of my father and Miranda, and indeed the legacy of my mother, how incredibly helpful and welcoming everyone who worked there was. Critical assistance came from our agent, Simon Dring, who has been at Badminton all his working life. For several years my father and I had met Simon for weekly meetings and now suddenly it was just me and him.

The only actual recognition that I made of my new position was to contact English Heraldry and ask them to go through the surprisingly complicated procedure of formally registering my right to stand in an election for hereditary peers sitting in the House of Lords, should one of the ninety-one currently there die. At one stage I thought I might do this but life at Badminton has rather taken over.

Some of the first friends who came to stay were Guy and Penny (who is always known as Barry) Morrison. By this time Barry had become a very successful interior decorator, so we were conscious of the importance of putting on a good show for her. Moreover, I had some making up to do: a few years earlier there had been a contretemps at The Cottage, which under Tracy and my management had not been a house famed for comfort. For various reasons I had been unable to fit Barry in for a shooting weekend, as Guy was not coming, and all other beds were taken by people who were shooting. Perhaps not the way to treat an old friend, and Barry expressed her disappointment, principally in jest, by responding, 'Well I didn't want to stay in your rat-infested hovel anyway!' For years after that we all referred to The Cottage as 'the hovel'.

Thus, on their first stay at Badminton under my and Georgia's management, we made sure that we put Guy and Barry in one of the very best bedrooms, so I was rather surprised when Guy discreetly approached me and said there was an odd smell in their room. I duly investigated and sure enough there was something truly malignant there. Panicked research ensued until the inevitable conclusion: a rat must have died under the floorboards and was rotting below their bed. As far as I know this has never happened again, but there was a rather splendid irony that Barry had been the person to suffer from the 'rat-infested hovel' in the otherwise luxurious surrounds of our new abode.

During the first few months of taking over Badminton, our first priority was to get married, and this took place in four stages. My divorce was finally completed a few days after we moved in and, for tax reasons, my advisers were keen that I should remarry immediately. We had a short ceremony where the only guests were Eddie and his faithful dog, 'Doggy', with Simon Dring and our butler Steve Matten acting as witnesses. About a month later we had a blessing with all members of our families and a few close friends staying in the house, and it was good to see the place coming alive again after the sad years of my father's decline. This was followed by a cocktail party in the garden for everyone who worked for us, and a good time seemed to be had by all.

In July 2018 we gave a party that was the *pièce de résistance* of our celebrations. A marquee was erected adjoining the house and, throughout the day, characters who have graced the pages of this book descended on Badminton. A lot of them arrived early to watch the England men's football team successfully move into the semi-finals of the World Cup, which massively enhanced the collective mood, and it was splendid walking from room to room encountering people of all ages screaming at the various televisions.

The guest list was deliberately inter-generational, with characters such as Taki, Shahriar Bakhtiar and Nicky Haslam representing the veteran class. Our children's friends and various members of the *jeunesse dorée* such as Sophia Hesketh and Marina Lambton added to the wild beauty of the occasion. The dress code was 'glam rave', which allowed plenty of interpretations, from Eighties clubbers to *haute couture*, and there was a massive display of colours and styles as the party began with drinks in the garden, followed by dinner in the marquee. Georgia and I had spent hours trying to perfect the placement, and the general buzz of conversation indicated our efforts had been rewarded. Georgia gave a brief speech, followed by Bobby's best man address, which was affectionately rude about his father.

The dancing was launched, preceded by a brief performance by The Listening Device to an ecstatic response from the assembled crowd. Then Johnson, and later Cousn, the DJ team comprising the son and nephew of Pearl Lowe and Danny Goffey, manned the decks and played frenzied dance music. We had installed quite a serious laser system, which made for a truly wild atmosphere in the ballroom for those in freak-out mode, while the marquee and the rest of the house and floodlit garden were available for anyone whose preference was cocktails and conversation. One-third of the guests were our children's friends, who seemed to be possessed of an almost demonic energy. George Kershaw and his wheelchair had adopted the usual position at the heart of the dance floor and soon he was accosted by an inebriated friend of my stepdaughter Hope. This girl announced that she could cure Kershaw's paralysis, and leapt on top of him, forgetting she was not wearing knickers as she gyrated, legs scissoring about his neck. Hope desperately hissed 'Vagina! Vagina!' at her friend, as she exhibited herself to Kershaw in graphic close-up. The girl remained unfazed, focused on finding out whether she had indeed brought about a Lazarus-like recovery in our friend. As Kershaw drew breath after this intervention, he was able to confirm her performance – alas – hadn't had the desired effect, remarking, 'but I think if you do it *again* it might work.'

When we finally got to bed it was about seven, and we could still hear the sound of a hardcore contingent of revellers below, music pounding up through the floorboards. Even when we got up a few hours later, there were still some stragglers awake, chatting by the fire or swimming in the pool. Georgia and I had perhaps lost the conversational fluidity of the previous evening, but were happy just to drift around and soak up the praise.

The band's performance at our wedding re-enthused all members. The month before, The Listening Device had performed at Danny Goffey and Pearl Lowe's small festival in their garden that they had organised because it was a fallow year for Glastonbury. We were delighted to perform alongside the local rock royalty, such as Brett Anderson of Suede, but the only problem was that the date coincided with the Beaufort Hunt puppy show and, having recently replaced my father as the Master of the Hunt, I felt obliged to attend. Finally, I managed to adjust our performance time so that I could rush away straight after the hound judging was completed, and the joint master, Ian Farquhar, issued the following explanation to those mystified by my sudden disappearance: 'I think he's gone to do something called a gig.' To date, The Listening Device have recorded four albums and also made a video, directed by Georgia's friend Matt Hammett Knott, and have achieved a cherished ambition of playing on one of the smaller stages at Glastonbury. In celebration of this, we decided to put together a greatest hits package. This, of course, is a slight misnomer as we have never had a hit, but the end result, which is entitled *Path to Redemption*, is a body of work of which I am proud.

My main priority since inheriting Badminton, though, has been to look after the estate and ensure it is in a good state for future generations. To begin with, I felt very daunted by the task. The costs of basic upkeep, heating and staff are enormous, and there is always the feeling that the main priority living here is to be a custodian, hoping to pass it on in at least as good condition as one inherited it. It means that, while one is the owner of an extremely valuable asset, extravagance that might be associated with such wealth has to be resisted. It is also not easy to adapt to the simple fact of being in such an unnaturally large house – change of any kind never comes easy: the Beaufort motto is *Mutare vel timere sperno*: I scorn to change or to fear.

My father had been backed up by his earnings in the art business, but the money I inherited had been shared with my siblings and Miranda, and of course the taxman. In short, we had to make the decision to go into the hospitality business. We are lucky to have Badminton Horse Trials as a base model for generating this type of income, and we have increased the number of other events taking place in the grounds to include such things as Tough Mudder, where 15,000 people take on a pre-built obstacle course in the park. It is the house, however, that is the bottomless pit for expenditure. Since 2018 we have allowed Badminton and the gardens to be used for occasional parties and weddings. The most exclusive events take place in our private wing of the house, and we tend to come as part of the package, so these occasions are rare but run on the basis that we know how to give a good party, and – without wishing to boast – people always seem to have a very good time here.

We have also increased the number of let shooting weekends in the house, still hosted by Georgia and me, where food, drink and comfort in the best tradition of Badminton are provided, while also giving the experience of a weekend in a family home, rather than the more colourless environment offered by some of our stately home competitors.

Alongside the hospitality, we have embarked in earnest on filming in the house. Having been warned by some friends that filming was disruptive and difficult at the very least, we have mostly been surprised by how conscientious film crews are about minimising damage and inconvenience. It is strange walking out of one's bathroom to find someone in headphones crouched behind the door telling you to be quiet but, in the patchwork of commercial activity that we are building for the house, filming has become an important income stream.

In our first few years in the house, we had two major television series filmed here: *Bridgerton*, one of the most successful series Netflix has ever made, and *The Pursuit of Love*, which was the first television drama to go into production in this country during the coronavirus pandemic. *The Pursuit of Love* was directed by Emily Mortimer. The cast also included other friends such as Dominic West and Annabel Mullion, so for much of the summer of 2020 we had close friends working and staying in and around the house.

On the whole I tend to avoid publicity, but when we were

approached by American *Vogue* to do a major piece on Badminton we thought it could be a subtle way of showing what we had to offer in the house. It was orchestrated by another Oxford friend of Georgia's, Plum Sykes, whose elegance and love of fashion hides a keen intelligence, and the legendary Hamish Bowles, who styled the whole piece. My daughter Bella and Georgia's daughter Hope, along with the daughters of my siblings, were all dressed by *Vogue* in a variety of suitable clothes and photographed at different spots in the house and garden, including a charming image of the girls all playing badminton in the North Hall, in reference to the sport being invented in the house.

I am, of course, aware that whatever efforts we make to turn the house into some sort of business, there will always be the possibility that politics could bash the whole project on its head. In this respect, the last few years have probably been the most traumatic I have experienced, starting with Brexit and all the chaos that continues to cause, then the election of a narcissistic man-child into the White House, followed by the near miss of a hard-left government led by Jeremy Corbyn. I am old enough to know that these things can change very fast.

CHAPTER 12

Guests

Georgia and I photographed as we prepare to enter my seventieth birthday party, where the dress code was 'Rave to the Grave'.

THE FILM CREWS temporarily taking over parts of the house are not the first people to have done so. Throughout the Second World War, Badminton was taken over, at the government's suggestion, by Mary's aunt, Queen Mary. There was strict secrecy to protect her from the Nazis, so hardly anyone knew for the whole five years she was there. Queen Mary arrived with a convoy of vans in October 1939, apparently with seventy pieces of luggage and fifty-five servants. The arrangement was that she would take over the entire house except for Master and Mary's bedrooms and personal sitting rooms. She kept three suitcases ready packed throughout the war with which to escape in the event of Nazis trying to kidnap her. I remember Master and Mary still talking about her twenty years later; it was a huge imposition – although they would never have said so publicly – and by all accounts, they were extremely relieved when she left.

Her presence did, however, stop the house being requisitioned as a hospital or barracks, which was a fate that befell some stately homes during the war. For her part, she displayed her gratitude by giving Master a full-length portrait of himself in full garter regalia by Oswald Birley, and this now hangs on the wall in my office.

I am sure Queen Mary would have been shocked to the core if she had witnessed my twenty-first-birthday party in the summer of 1973. Master decided to celebrate fifty years of living at Badminton by having a week of five parties: one for his friends, one for the hunt, one for the estate workers, one for the tenant farmers and then finally one for my twenty-first birthday and Monster's eighteenth. A marquee was erected in the garden, and, for our party, my mother incorporated some magnificent flower arrangements, and we also had use of the ballroom and some of the rooms in the house. We hired a rock band called Bitch, meant to be the next big thing; Master was delighted as he assumed their name carried some hunting connotation. That night, however, he went out to dinner and returned when the band were in full cry, and became seriously worried that the vibrations from the sheer volume of the music would damage the chandeliers.

By the time we were in our early twenties, Monster and I had built quite a circle of friends but were still rather reluctant to have them to stay at home. We weren't entirely comfortable in the way that we behaved with our parents, contrasting with the sillier antics expressed to the full among our friends. This prompted my father to joke, 'Either you're ashamed of your parents or you're a bugger,' to which I was gifted the simple response of, 'Well Daddy, I'm not a bugger.'

When eventually we did succumb, the dam was well and truly breached and the house was hardly ever without young guests, who realised how lucky we were to have such informal and relaxed parents. Our friends particularly enjoyed the eccentric sides of my mother, who would never sit down, striding around waving her arms about, normally with both a drink and cigarette. My father was also deceptively funny, and in some ways everyone's fantasy: he was good looking and successful in business.

Queen Mary was not the only distinguished guest at Badminton. During the Second World War, Eleanor Roosevelt joined her there during her home-front tour of Britain, and Emperor Haile Selassie of Ethiopia also visited Queen Mary while he was exiled and living in Bath. The Queen was Master's guest each year for thirty years, for the Horse Trials. She always stayed in the same room, which was joined to Prince Philip's, her Protection Officer always sitting on the same velvet chair outside the door whenever she was there. We have recently redecorated the bedroom where Prince Philip slept, calling it the Edinburgh Room in his memory.

The Queen and Prince Philip were often accompanied by

their children, the Queen Mother and Princess Margaret, all of whom would attend church services with Master and then go for rides in the park. Watching the cross-country from farm trailers or a rug beside the lake, the Royal Family would mingle with spectators – something I think, sadly, would no longer be possible these days.

While my parents lived at Badminton, Imran Khan visited a couple of times, Tracy and I having stayed with him in Pakistan during our honeymoon. Imran is probably the greatest cricketer Pakistan has ever produced, and since leaving Oxford he had spent his summers in England playing county cricket, which had given him the opportunity to enjoy a highly successful playboy lifestyle, before going back home in the winter to Pakistan. There was no doubt this was where his heart lay, but he understandably also enjoyed the freedoms of London, where his success with girls seemed limitless.

When Imran stayed at Badminton, he played in my annual cricket match against the village. On the first occasion he made an effortless century but on the second, perhaps distracted by a girl in the crowd, he did less well and skied an easy catch. This prompted a wit in the village team to bellow, 'Imran Khan, caught village idiot, bowled village idiot!', causing much mirth on the pitch.

During the same visit my mother was lying in bed in the morning when there was a knock on the door and the house-keeper, rather overwhelmed by having a celebrity guest in the house, came in and said, 'Excuse me, Your Grace, but the dark-skinned gentleman is in bed with one of the young ladies.' My mother mildly reprimanded her for this unnecessary indiscretion, but half an hour later the housekeeper returned undaunted. 'Your Grace, I thought I should tell you that the dark-skinned gentleman is now in bed with *another* of the young ladies.'

As well as being a great all-rounder, Imran had also been the best captain his country had ever had, moulding a group of talented individuals into a cohesive team unit, and it was fascinating to see the level of adulation this had created for him. When Tracy and I were staying with him in Pakistan, we were in the car with him in urban areas of the country and, throughout the journey, people spotted him as the car stopped in traffic. Within seconds the car would be surrounded by people clamouring for his attention. In more rural areas we would arrive at our destination in the evening, eat and then go to bed, but by morning there would be lines of people outside the hotel wanting to get a glimpse of the great man. Imran would oblige them briefly, lying regally outside as the crowds filed past. He seemed totally unfazed even when the car was surrounded, but it was mildly alarming and probably not dissimilar to Beatlemania in 1960s Britain.

The most extraordinary thing about Imran was his belief in his own destiny. This was evident in the cricketing sphere when he was pulled out of retirement to captain Pakistan in their bid to win the World Cup in 1992, and from this moment on he always preceded any reference to the competition with 'when' we win, rather than 'if'. Despite this, the team played appallingly in the early stages of the tournament and reached a point where they not only had to win all their remaining games but were also reliant on various other matches going the right way. When he was interviewed quite aggressively about this, he stood his ground defiantly and one could sense that his belief was still intact, countering the questions with a confident, 'We'll see.' And, of course, they went on to win the trophy.

After this victory Imran gave up cricket and initially devoted his time to building a cancer hospital in Pakistan in honour of his mother, before moving on to full-time politics. He still used to come to England, and one weekend at Badminton he told Tracy that he believed it was his destiny to be the leader of his country. Tracy was convinced by this vision, not least because his attitude to America's malign influence in the world conformed to hers, but I was more cynical, thinking the machinations and corruption of Pakistan politics would always find a way of thwarting him. For many years this proved to be the case but in 2018 he finally achieved his cherished ambition.

Such is the unpredictability of Pakistan's politics that he was deposed in 2022 on spurious grounds and recently sentenced to three years in jail on trumped-up corruption charges. There is a cruel irony that this is the very crime he has devoted the last twenty-five years of his life trying to eliminate.

In the twenty years that Imran was in politics before he became Prime Minister there were often newspaper reports that he was about to go into some sort of coalition with the ruling party, and on one of his visits to England I asked him about this. His answer left me in no doubt that, as leader of an anti-corruption party, he was not prepared to compromise. 'They are criminals, Bunter. How can I work with criminals?' When Pakistan won the World Cup, they toured England the following summer and Imran asked us round to his flat to meet 'my team'. What was striking about this was the incredible loyalty all these players felt towards him, even though he had by now retired.

He has a sense of humour and a rather splendid, if slightly controlled, booming laugh. He is, however, a rather literal man and I can remember him being shocked by Tim Hanbury's bad-taste party piece discussing his daughters' sex lives in excessive detail, albeit with a great deal of affection. The rest of us roared with laughter but Imran didn't get the joke at all, confiding afterwards, 'the relationship between father and daughter is such a beautiful thing that I find those comments really quite offensive'.

I always assumed Imran's forays to England would gradually decline and that he would eventually return to Pakistan for some sort of arranged marriage. There was no doubt, however, that he was still conflicted, and in 1995 he surprised everyone by announcing his engagement to Jemima Goldsmith, daughter of the tycoon Jimmy Goldsmith and over twenty years his junior. This was a true love match, with two strong characters having real respect for each other, which they have retained to this day, but the cultural and geographical differences always made it unlikely that the union could survive its course. They were married for nine years, divorcing in 2004.

Some years earlier, Elizabeth Hurley had rented a house about five miles from Badminton. I somehow contrived to invite her to dinner, and it was noticeable how many of my friends suddenly found that they too were available, including my father, who previously had shown only modest enthusiasm about dining at The Cottage. There was lots of laughter, and I was struck by how unlike an actress Elizabeth was, cultivating her inner Sloane rather than street cred. She spoke more like a dormitory captain at a girls' boarding school than a Hollywood star, sprinkling about phrases like 'goody gumdrops'. Sadly, the lease on her house expired shortly afterwards, but these characteristics were again in evidence when we were both at a cricket match where rain stopped play, and she insisted everyone played rounders instead, and then proceeded to gallop around like an attractive but demented gym mistress.

Badminton has always kept a relaxed air for guests, my family perhaps being particularly laid back. Often, I'd be there when my parents had their friends to stay. My father's best friend was Michael Tree, who had a sort of lazy wisdom, and I remember him once sauntering over to me as we were standing in line shooting and saying wearily, 'Sometimes I feel I've spent half my life staring at woods waiting for birds to come out.'

Michael was also the most terrible gossip. Once, he was telephoned and informed of the death of an acquaintance. He put the phone down immediately, leaving the bearer of bad news nonplussed. The latter concluded that he must have been rather tactless in his delivery and rang my father saying, 'Poor old Michael, I never knew how fond he was of Virginia . . .' My father, however, knew the animal better and explained that Michael was not really that upset; he just didn't want to waste a single moment before passing the news on to others.

Both Michael and my father were friends of Sunny Blandford, who subsequently became the 11th Duke of Marlborough, and they became obsessed with Sunny's father Bert (as everyone called him) Marlborough on their visits to Blenheim Palace. Bert was a man of legendary rudeness combined with a modest element of wit, and whenever he mumbled what he regarded as a humorous insult he used to follow it up with a derisory high-pitched snort, just to make sure everyone got the joke. Strangely, the modern branches of the Churchill family share this snorting trait, so it may be hereditary.

On one occasion Bert was sitting next to a society beauty at dinner, and after the first course she lit up a cigarette. He asked her why, and she replied defensively that she liked smoking. Quick as a flash Bert retorted, 'Well I like fucking, but I don't do it in the middle of dinner,' followed by the inevitable snort. Another time, a Greek, who was courting Bert's daughter Sarah, requested an audience with him and asked very formally if he could have her hand in marriage. Bert replied, 'Well, you've had just about everything else, you might as well have her hand.' The snort was perhaps extra loud this time. He was also not beyond being a little caddish and, one day out shooting, he pointed to a cottage by the woods, saying that he used to keep a mistress there and pop in and see to her in the middle of a day's sport, adding by way of explanation, 'There was never much to shoot in that drive anyway.'

In the 1950s Bert's cousin Randolph Churchill, son of Sir Winston, asked if he could stay the night at Blenheim as he wanted to do some research in the family archives for the book he was writing. At dinner it was just the two of them in the large dining room and, as they were about to sit down, the butler appeared wheeling a television set in and began the lengthy process of tuning necessary in those days. Randolph was rather shocked by this breach of etiquette and made his feelings known in a rather pompous manner. 'Honestly Bert, I really don't think this is the sort of behaviour you'd expect from men of our stature,' to which Bert retorted without embarrassment, 'Well it's better than listening to your boring conversation.'

Tony Lambton was equally unembarrassed about being rude to people, even if they were his guest, being especially rude about their families. When Philip Naylor-Leyland was courting his daughter Isabella, who he subsequently married, he was a bit nervous about his first meeting with Tony. This was exacerbated during lunch when Tony didn't address a single word to him until the pudding arrived, whereupon he pronounced, 'Your father was the most ghastly man, wasn't he?'

Although Tony's behaviour could seem cruel, it was more often based in an extraordinary sense of the absurd. On one occasion his neighbour in Italy, Mark Getty, came to lunch at his Tuscan villa Cetinale, bringing with him the professor who had taught him philosophy at Oxford and the historian Andrew Roberts. The professor did not blend that naturally into our rather rowdy group, but Andrew did some sterling work having an intellectual conversation with him throughout the meal. Tony couldn't resist interfering with this and butted in, 'Andrew, can I ask you something?' Andrew replied politely, saying that he was talking to the professor, but Tony persevered, repeating his request. This time Andrew was a bit exasperated, but again explained the reason for his not answering. Still determined, Tony butted in for a third time and Andrew had no choice but to apologise to the professor and enquire what it was that Tony wanted. Everyone was then rather surprised to hear their host asking, 'I was just wondering how many times you go to the lavatory every day?'

Many of my parents' friends were more conventionally polite although just as interesting. Judy Gendel was a firm favourite and she'd often spend weekends at The Cottage when my parents lived there during the 1970s. She was both funny and intelligent and also had a real interest in young people, while often sharing their timekeeping and not getting up until lunchtime. At that stage in life, I generally found it quite difficult to talk to people outside my own age group, but she made it a real pleasure and it was very sad when she died prematurely a few years later. Another regular was my mother's brother Christopher Thynne and his wife Antonia. He was a few years younger than my parents and on the fringes of the upper-class hippy group who hung out with the likes of Mick Jagger in the swinging Sixties. With his eccentric clothes and enjoyment of the occasional drink, he was a splendid guest to be around. He had very little money and made his living from being a society photographer, but, despite being talented and having the contacts to get the work, he was also prone to such basic errors as forgetting to put a film in the camera and never achieved the prominence of his contemporaries such as Patrick Lichfield.

At the other end of artistic success was Lucian Freud, who was attached to the Marlborough Gallery in its early days and remained a great friend of my father's until he died. Lucian never left London except during the Notting Hill carnival, when the noise outside his house became intolerable, and those three days he always came to Badminton for the weekend. He often brought a girl with him, normally considerably younger, and he spoke in a very quiet voice that disguised a slightly vicious wit. I got to know him quite well and sometimes used to bump into him in London. On one occasion we were talking in a drinking club when a star-struck woman came over and began assailing him with rather tiresome questions. She eventually asked if he had known Jackie Kennedy, to which he replied in the affirmative. She followed up by asking if he had found her attractive. Lucian said he didn't really, but then added in his rather quiet voice, 'But there *was* something about the way she climbed over the back of the car when her husband was killed.' I was surprised by this bad-taste answer, but the next time I saw the film of the shooting I noticed a cat-like eroticism in how she moved in that moment of desperation.

In contrast to the laid-back approach of my parents, sometimes I have been a guest in much more formal circumstances. In my early twenties, I visited my friend Sarah Astor at her parents' house, Tillypronie in Scotland, an experience rather like what I imagine being a guest at Balmoral must be like. Staying there involved attending reeling parties almost every night. I had no idea about the complicated manoeuvres required for the different reels, but assumed I could bluff my way round this. Sadly, within the first two bars of 'Dashing White Sergeant' I realised that mindlessly leaping up and down in the air was not going to fool anyone; kilted males, keen to show off their skills, didn't need a bumbling oaf crashing around and getting in their way. Some grew quite aggressive, growling at me to get off the dance floor, and I decided to bow to the inevitable and accept that my seduction skills on this particular battlefield were not to be seen to their best advantage.

The father of Sarah's cousin William Astor died when he was a teenager. And William bought a manor house in Berkshire where some fairly unruly behaviour was possible in the absence of parental invigilation. He retained a butler and cook, and there was also a pheasant shoot, which, while obviously quite rare for a young man in his early twenties, provided a most enjoyable framework for his guests to operate in.

One of the regulars there was Mark Shand. Mark was a charismatic character, loved by girls, but never totally reliable. I stayed with William just after John Lennon had been shot, and he was furious that Mark had not turned up on Friday night for a shooting weekend, or even left a message to explain his absence. The next day we were getting ready to climb into the Land Rovers when Mark suddenly appeared in a taxi from Heathrow. He apologised profusely, saying he was meant to be coming back from New York three days ago but every time he walked past the Dakota Building where the shooting had taken place, he was accosted by girls asking if he knew John, and every time he couldn't quite resist inventing a story around the pretence that he had, which invariably meant that he ended up in bed with the girl, further delaying his departure. An adventurer, Mark eventually made his name writing the bestseller *Travels on My Elephant*, the story of his journey across India riding his beloved Tara, and then devoted the rest of his life to campaigning for elephants. Tragically, he was killed in his early sixties in 2014 in a freak accident involving a collision with a revolving door in a New York hotel.

I don't think my reputation is as eccentric as that of some of my friends, but I am perhaps known for my clumsiness, which, at 6 foot 6 inches tall, is hard to hide. At the summer party of the much-loved matriarch of the Goldsmith family, Annabel, I met Conrad Black, then the owner of the *Daily Telegraph*, making a memorable impression. Every year Annabel gives this annual party in the garden of her Richmond home, comprising a wide variety of people including royalty, politicians, media people, sportsmen and friends of all ages. The garden has a network of paths lined with box hedges about three foot high, and one year these had burning candles on top of them at ten-metre intervals. I was ambling along one of these paths when I suddenly heard my friend Taki's voice from the other side of the hedge calling me over. I looked up and saw that he was standing there with Conrad Black and his wife, the journalist Barbara Amiel. I waved at them, but initially was slightly reluctant to go to the trouble of negotiating the hedge. I was persuaded by the siren-like beckoning of Barbara, who I had always found extremely attractive, and set about the task. I placed my left foot over the hedge and then tried to follow it with my right, but, however hard I tried, it seemed to have somehow got stuck. I kicked and pulled and finally was on solid ground, and walked rather proudly up to them, looking admiringly at Barbara, but these thoughts were interrupted by Conrad calling out agitatedly, 'Waiter . . . Waiter! Please can you come here. My suit is covered in wax.'

I slowly realised why I'd had so much difficulty getting over the hedge, as my foot must have got caught on one of the candles, and every time I attempted to release it by kicking, I had sprayed Conrad with another load of wax. By the time I saw him he looked like some sort of leopard. There was little doubt that his suit was ruined, but he accepted my apologies very graciously. Unfortunately, a week later I was at a party given at Wormsley by the Getty family and there was an incredible fireworks display. I was rather over-inebriated that night, and also tend to find fireworks pointless at the best of times, so I decided to try to amuse myself, and the girl I was standing with, by shouting out some babyish comments laced with swear-words. This was of course only moderately funny and, when I finally gave my audience some respite from this performance, I looked around, and there, directly behind me, was Conrad. I couldn't help thinking that if he hadn't thought I was a blithering idiot the previous week, he surely did now.

This embarrassing experience diminishes in comparison to when Tony Blair, who was Prime Minister at the time, was a guest at Centinale. During one of my last holidays there, there was great excitement when the Italian neighbours, the Strozzis, rang up and said they had Blair staying and were wondering if they could bring him over to see the villa. They were immediately all asked to lunch, and Tony Lambton instructed his grandson, Fred, and me to stand in a military-style line to greet Blair. Eventually, Blair and his entourage arrived, and the first thing he requested was the use of the bathroom, to which he was duly shown, and the three of us continued our vigil outside in silence.

He took some considerable time to conduct operations, and we just stood there feeling more and more sheepish, until Tony (Lambton) suddenly turned to one of the body-guards and said, 'I think he must have the most appalling diarrhoea, don't you?' I was also a bit surprised when I later overheard Tony describing someone to Blair as 'smelling like a mule's arse', this rather unusual simile causing a flicker of surprise on the countenance of the normally unflappable Prime Minister.

Blair had walked the five miles from the Strozzis, but his four-year-old son Leo had been brought over by car, and his next request was that he could have a quick swim with him before lunch. He was duly shown the swimming pool and we all left him to enjoy this private family moment, but my brother Johnson has always found contact with celebrities irresistible, and he was staying put. He dived into the pool and began swimming up and down, and every time he passed Blair, he fired a question at him about Iraq. Blair, of course, was normally the master of deft evasion, but on this occasion he was imprisoned by the fact that he was bouncing his son up and down in the water, and there was no escape from the cascade of relentless questions.

During the years that I was married to Tracy, we spent many family holidays in Cetinale, mixing our friends with Tony and Clare's. An essential feature of the Cetinale experience was Jasper and Camilla Guinness, who also lived in Italy. Camilla has a splendidly deep voice, a slightly vampish look and a sense of humour that makes her very effective at pinpointing the minor frailties in people that make one like them all the more. Having moved nearby, they were regular guests and Jasper, with an almost childlike hatred of going to bed early, guaranteed some very enjoyable discussions that tended to last way into the night and incorporate more alcohol than strictly advisable.

Jerry Hall was an occasional visitor to Cetinale and she also asked Tracy and me to stay at the chateau in the Loire Valley that she shared with Mick Jagger. On arrival, we were greeted by Mick and the sight of about four or five hot-air balloons. All the guests got into the balloons excitedly, but I suffer from vertigo. Gripping the sides, I tried to pretend in front of the extremely cool group of people that I was enjoying the view, not daring to share my terror. Everyone else loved it but I was extremely relieved when the basket lurched back down on to solid ground.

Mick's creative flair stands out, but other hosts are memorable for their eccentricity. As a result of Tracy's environmental and wildlife interests, we visited John Aspinall in the late 1980s. John had made money from casinos, ploughing much of it into a number of zoos. He had an element of a Bond villain about him, and his reputation became still more controversial when several keepers were killed by his animals. In the late 1960s, Annabel Goldsmith's then-eleven-year-old son Robin Birley was also mauled by one of his tigers, leaving the bones on one side of his face crushed, and he had to have ongoing cosmetic surgery.

No doubt Aspinall preferred animals to human beings; in fact, he regarded man as little more than a sophisticated animal species. His favourites were the predators, and this admiration extended into the human sphere; he hugely respected Jimmy Goldsmith for his aggressive business practices. Strangely, he also had regard for aristocrats such as me, basically seeing our survival as part of some Darwinian selective-breeding programme. When we stayed with Aspinall, Tracy was in the early stages of pregnancy, and I was a bit concerned by her insistence that she frolic with the young tiger cubs, but thankfully no damage was done.

While the Aspinall tiger visit was a one-off, an annual mainstay for me for twenty-five years was the McEwen New Year, where I loved being a guest of my friend Sophie and her family. New Year in Scotland is taken much more seriously, than it is south of the border. The McEwens are descended from an old Scottish clan and, perhaps because they are so aware of this heritage, were more than happy to indulge in the hard drinking that the festivities required. Their finances were slowly falling on hard times, and Bardrochat, the large house where we all gathered for New Year, was an expense that they couldn't strictly speaking afford. This may have explained the slight feeling of melancholy rippling not far from the surface in the family, even when they were in full celebration mode, but when put in the melting pot alongside generally riotous behaviour, a lingering Catholicism and their artistic and musical flair, it made for an irresistible combination.

While Eck McEwen offered a lively atmosphere of music and booze, his wife Cecilia, a beautiful Austrian aristocrat, probably drank slightly less than the rest of us, but, despite having a relatively petite body, she certainly needed no additional inputs to encourage her to make a great deal of noise. Nicknamed 'The Fiery Furnace', she was to be avoided if her temper went even slightly off-kilter. She was, however, much loved by all of them and there was something rather endearing about the way they always referred to 'Mama', which encouraged me as a matter of priority to bray that word like a donkey as a form of greeting to her every year. This was probably not particularly amusing but very much in the absurd spirit of the occasion.

Along with her brothers Dumbie and Hugo, Sophie was a vital part of the jigsaw and could be relied upon to be the last person to bed every night. With an infectious laugh, albeit of a volume that her mother complained was not entirely ladylike, she brought a wonderful enthusiasm to any conversation.

There were always about twenty people staying in the house for New Year, with other locals coming for the New Year's Eve party itself, including Houston Shaw-Stewart, who always brought along his best friend Bobby Corbett. Houston had been decorated in the Korean War and then in the main lived the life of a landowner on his estate. He held traditional views, but was certainly not as conventional as his father, who he had felt it necessary to take aside once and warn about one of his shooting guests. Houston's friend was gay, and he was worried that, if discovered inadvertently, there might come some sort of outburst. When the guests started to arrive, the man in question was wearing a tweed suit and a tie, and his father seemed to be getting on especially well with him until he was suddenly overheard leaning over and whispering confidentially, 'By the way old boy, I suggest you watch out . . . there's a bugger coming to stay.'

Houston's friend Bobby was such an improbable character that he would not have looked out of place even in the most satirical Evelyn Waugh novel. He had a bright-red face and terrible pock-marked skin, probably because of drink, although Tony Lambton was always determined that it was because he refused to use shaving cream. The most remarkable thing about him was his way of speaking, so fast as to render him almost impossible to understand. The first time I met him I remember sitting next to him at dinner in a state of total incomprehension, but in fact it was rather like learning a foreign language, and after a few meetings it all began to make sense. Once I had achieved this breakthrough, I realised he was not only incredibly funny, with almost every sentence a gem, but also very cultured. Bobby was also a friend of my mother's and used to organise tours around Scottish castles and houses with her. She too was not averse to the occasional drink and shared his ability to make a great deal of noise. On more than one occasion they were asked by irate hoteliers to quieten down. The one similarity all the guests shared was our capacity to consume enormous quantities of alcohol. When I got home every year my father tended to comment that he had never seen me looking so ill, but my consumption was relatively modest compared to some of the other champions there.

Unruly behaviour seems to run seamlessly into the younger generations. In 2000, my niece Francesca celebrated her eighteenth-birthday party by the newly built circular swimming pool my father had designed. It was a warm evening, and the fountain in the centre of the pool was shooting water high into the air, creating a spectacular setting for the evening celebrations. One of the guests was

Prince Harry, who was a contemporary of Francesca's and had come over from his father's house, Highgrove, which lies about five miles from Badminton. Initially he seemed to blend in quite well, but he suddenly became possessed, lifted a girl over his shoulder, walked over to the swimming pool and hurled her in. There was a predictable outburst of laughter from the other guests and Harry, pleased with this reaction, continued to indulge himself by repeating the performance with several other girls, one after another. There seemed to be a law of diminishing returns in terms of audience response, but relentlessly he kept on with his mission; he rather reminded me of a man picking up sacks of coal and chucking them on to the back of a lorry.

The problem was that none of the girls had brought other clothes to change into, and had the performance continued the party would have been ruined. I was a bit overawed by the fact of his royal status and was rather slow to stop him, but luckily my father's butler Steve was there. Steve told Harry in no uncertain terms that he should stop at once. As the soaking girls were taken up to the house to borrow some clothes, Johnson came up and, imitating the voice of J. R. Ewing from the American soap, *Dallas*, said, 'We gotta be real careful that nothin' happens to that boy's older brother . . . real careful.'

CHAPTER 13

The Horse Trials

The photograph of Georgia in the North Hall at Badminton
that appeared in American *Vogue*.

POLITICAL CHANGE WAS always looked on warily by my father and the Dukes before him because the future of Badminton was invariably a concern. Many tactics have been devised to keep the wolf from the door. Indisputably, the most successful venture, born not out of schemes but genuine interest, is the Horse Trials that Master started in 1949. Thanks to Master's interest in riding, he created a legacy that continues to flourish, spurred on by the disastrous performance of the British Three-Day Event team at the 1948 London Olympics. His logic was simple: it was absurd that the British had done so badly when the hunting field provided the perfect place to prepare riders from an early age. As a result of the Horse Trials, the British team has performed extremely well and continues to do so right up to the present day, including winning the gold medal at the 2021 Tokyo Olympics. It has been the centrepiece of the year at Badminton ever since, growing into a massive event, with an attendance in excess of a hundred and fifty thousand. Every year, the house fills to capacity with a whole variety of people, whose numbers swell on the cross-country day with a huge buffet lunch.

Not surprisingly, I learnt to ride from the earliest age possible. As a child, from day to day I wanted to do nothing more than just muck about, but being at Badminton meant that riding was never far from the mix. After an early inability to stay aboard a pony, an exceptionally quiet animal was purchased to get my confidence back, and I used to ride it to the end of the garden, barely able to rouse a trot, and then benefit from a little more enthusiasm as we turned for home. One day I was going through this procedure, wondering if it might be a little easier with a slightly keener animal. I got to the end of the garden and gave the pony an almighty kick, and was pleased to find this had been effective and that we were travelling at a fast canter, even a gallop. The trouble was that I think it had been stung by a wasp and when we reached the house it continued galloping and then swung left and headed towards the substantial ha-ha surrounding the gardens. Even at this speed the only option was to bale out, which I somehow managed without incurring a serious injury, but as a result of this moment of sheer terror my riding career was once again put on the back burner.

By the time I reached prep-school age my father had set up daily lunchtime riding lessons for me with his coach, a Hungarian Olympic medallist with limited English skills. I certainly did not enjoy these sessions and my enduring memory is of the coach shouting, 'Trotty, trotty, trotty' as I approached very small obstacles at which I regularly seemed to fall off. Eventually, with my equine skills failing to develop as hoped, my riding career was suspended once again.

Following the confidence-shattering experiences of early childhood I was given a cob when I was about fifteen, which we called Hippo. Hippo was as fat a horse as I have ever seen but did miraculously heave his massive frame over fences, and I began hunting. After Hippo, it was time to move on to something a little classier, and a horse called Confetto was produced, but, despite being a good jumper, he quickly learnt how to ignore my instructions, as well as being impossible to stop. This was obviously no fun and, just as I was wavering again and thinking I would give the sport up, my father sent me for a week of riding lessons with Frank Weldon, who had competed against him at Badminton and now ran the Horse Trials. Over that week my horsemanship was transformed. I was never going to become a rider of the highest standard, but with the right horse I could really enjoy hunting, which I did for nearly twenty years.

My father employed the riding coach because he had taken up three-day eventing himself and was steadily improving, coming seventh at Badminton in 1958 on his horse Countryman. In 1959 Monster and I were allowed to watch the event for the first time, but he went the wrong way in his dressage and finished well down the order, which everyone thought had put paid to his chances. It was an exceptionally wet year, and in the cross-country element all the other riders elected to go very slowly in the testing conditions, while he took the view that wet ground out hunting never required such caution so there was no reason for it to do so here, and after a blemish-free and very fast round he found himself in the lead. Show-jumping was always his weaker discipline and he knocked a fence down, while the well-known eventer Sheila Willcox, lying second, didn't, and pipped him for victory, winning for the third consecutive year. This was despite Monster and me screaming from the stands at the top of our voices, 'Knock it down, knock it down' in an unashamedly partisan way, behaviour that even the stern disciplinarian Nanny Nelson allowed to pass. My father never rode at Badminton again but I'm sure he was disappointed by this near miss – nobody remembers a runner-up.

The 1984 Horse Trials was the first year my parents were in Badminton after Master had died. The whole family were supplied with 'Rover' stickers for our cars, which meant we could drive around the event, a privilege much appreciated by the lazier guests. It was very wet, which meant the crossing points over the course became exceptionally muddy, and when driving around it was necessary sometimes to take a bit of a run-up to negotiate this hazard. Johnson entrusted the driving of his car to a friend, who, unaware of the significance of whistles being blown by mounted stewards, drove flat out over the crossing point and was unlucky enough to go straight into a horse and knock it to the ground. Luckily, the horse was not seriously injured, but it did mean that the event had to stop for half an hour, which was very disruptive.

When my father was informed of this he was not pleased, but his real anger was slow to ferment and did not hit a peak until he got back to the house. Johnson had the sense to make himself scarce, and the only people my father could find were Eddie and some of his guests, including the Argentinian playboy Luis Basualdo, sitting in the library, obviously completely uninterested in any equestrian activity. My father had always loathed Basualdo, suspecting him of leaking stories to the gossip columns about the family, and the sight of him casually lolling there lit his fuse. He was still holding the stick he carried while walking the course and he suddenly found himself thrashing out at Basualdo, who, having initially thought he was being approached by the Duke for some friendly banter, was left cowering, spluttering, 'David, I am your buddy. David, I am your buddy,' in his heavy accent as my father stormed from the room.

My friend Dave Ker, who stays every year for the Horse Trials, loves driving around the course in his Range Rover, with conversation taking on a predominantly gossip-based flavour. He is often teased that what he really likes about these sessions is that, when members of the public see this large, well-dressed man in such a vehicle, they assume he is the Duke. He too, however, is inclined to be distracted by anything royal and on one occasion he saw Prince William walking the course with a group of his friends, whereupon he dropped any semblance of ducal dignity, leapt out of the car and sprinted towards him at a speed one would not have thought possible for a man of his substantial girth.

My father also had friends who would come every year, including Guy Knight, or 'The Major' as he was universally known. Guy was a suave figure who my father had met when he was in the army, and really liked to use this gathering as an excuse to play endless games of backgammon. Even now when I play the game, I hear some of the catchphrases he tirelessly used. Guy also enjoyed a joke by repetition and loved to remind me of something that happened when I was a teenager and had gone out pigeon shooting: how when I returned my father asked how I'd got on and I proudly announced that I'd killed ten, to which he reasonably enquired if I had put them in the kitchen. The reality was that in my ignorance I had not bothered to pick them up and just left their corpses strewn all over the field. When my father expressed mild annoyance and asked why I had not done this, I said something along the lines of, 'Not much point, Dad' – a phrase Guy used to repeat mindlessly whenever I saw him thereafter.

When Guy came shooting with Master, he would make trouble by going up to him after a drive and saying in his smooth voice, 'Bunter tells me we're not bothering to pick the birds up today, is that right?' Master had a low opinion of my sporting pedigree at the best of times and bellowed, 'Of course not!', looking at me as if I were a halfwit, as Guy walked away quietly saying, 'Yes, I thought that couldn't be right.' The annoying thing was that by the time the next season came round, Master had forgotten, and Guy was able to repeat the whole performance all over again.

When Prince William and Harry were boys, they too attended the Horse Trials. Once, my father drove them and Princess Diana around in his Land Rover, Harry sitting on his lap helping him steer. Another year, Princess Diana came to lunch during the Trials. My father, who had spent all day with her, later said that he had found it quite hard going, as she was like a child. When she later joined up with my friends and me, that childishness seemed very much part of her charm, and she fell into hysterics when Dave Ker described someone as having a bush like a burst sofa, and then again when Peter Jansen suddenly pointed at an aeroplane flying overhead and said in his rough Australian accent, 'Hey ma'am, let's hope they don't let the toilets out on us,' a joke of which the only merit was out-and-out lavatorial vulgarity.

Later, we were all a bit hungry. We headed for the kitchen, and I gave Diana a spoon and plonked some leftovers from lunch on to the table. This prompted Dave to say in joke pomposity, 'I think Her Royal Highness might prefer a proper plate and cutlery, Harry,' but in fact I felt the very informality of the whole thing was a bit of a treat and a welcome escape from her ivory tower.

I didn't know Diana well, but we shared many mutual friends, so sometimes our paths would cross. Diana regularly used to take her boys to lunch with Annabel Goldsmith at her house by Richmond Park. On one occasion, Annabel's daughter Jemima and niece Sophia Pilkington were playing with Prince William, who was about eleven years old, and one of them rugby-tackled him and brought him to the ground. At this moment Diana came around the corner and said in a mock-nanny voice, 'Hey, be careful of the future king of England's goolies.' There was something about her use of the word 'goolies', rare today even in slang, and the unspoken reference to the dynastic importance of said items, that carried a naïve charm.

Annabel was something of a mentor to Diana and on one occasion, perhaps influenced by her husband Jimmy's new-found environmentalism, advised her that nowadays she needed to be very considerate about what she ate. Diana looked up from her plate and replied rather earnestly, 'Don't worry, I'm very careful what I put down my hatch.' As well as having a comical ring, it was again rather surprising that she had used such an unusual word, although possibly this was indicative of her general attitude to eating.

A few years later I was placed next to Diana at a dinner party. At the time, large parts of the press were intent on presenting her as wayward and difficult, and I didn't know exactly how appropriate it would be to question her on the subject. I therefore began tentatively, but she was not embarrassed at all and said, 'To think of all the things I've done for that family,' before launching into more general complaints about the media: 'I can't understand why they keep linking me with rugger players.'

Above all, she possessed a real compassion that the rest of the buttoned-up Royal Family could never match. Her friend Rosa Monckton told me that, as godmother to her Down's Syndrome child, Diana was attentive way beyond the call of duty, and with no cameras ever present, adding that her irrational moments were normally triggered by a fear of desertion, a fate that had stalked her throughout her life. Her ability to reach out to all sorts of people was confirmed to me by Imran Khan when he described how Jemima had arranged some invaluable publicity for his hospital project in Pakistan by persuading Diana to visit. Imran said that she displayed an astonishing lack of knowledge about what was going on in the world, but when she actually spoke or sat down with the patients it was extraordinary how they reacted to her, seeming to discover a sort of inner peace that they had not had before. Twenty-five years on, her enigmatic fascination endures.

Unlike Master, my parents were not close friends of the Queen, and the security implications of her driving around the park were becoming increasingly onerous, so the tradition of her staying every year ceased. In 1998, however, it was the fiftieth anniversary of the start of the event, and she agreed to stay on a one-off basis. We were all taken up in the excitement of this, not least Matthew Carr and Johnson, who both happened to arrive exhausted after a week of unusually hard living. Nonetheless, they still wanted to be swept up in her aura, and when we were having pre-dinner drinks in the library, Matthew was to be seen hovering close by, before suddenly swooping towards her and announcing theatrically, 'Ma'am, it really is absolutely wonderful that you are here,' and then gliding away as swiftly as he had arrived.

The Queen could only blink after this unusual welcome, but just as she was recovering her composure Johnson appeared. He was more controlled in his adulation and asked a question about Prince William's gap-year travels in Africa. The Queen launched into a detailed description of the itinerary of William and his friend James Meade, but after a few moments Johnson's hangover kicked in again and he totally lost concentration, her words sounding more like a buzzing mosquito than actual diction. After about thirty seconds he came out of this trance to hear her finishing off the story, saying, 'And after that he's returning home to go back to university.'

Johnson had by this time totally lost the thread of what she was saying, and gambled unsuccessfully by asking, 'Er . . . you mean Prince William, Ma'am?', following which he got a really fairly angry retort from the Queen, who snapped, 'No! James Meade!' I suspect she left harbouring doubts about the intellectual capacities of some of the younger members of our family.

On another occasion the Queen came to lunch on the Sunday of the Horse Trials and presented the prizes. It happened to be her birthday and everyone staying in the house stood in a circle to bow and shake hands with her. When she reached Guy Knight, he laid on his famously suave charm and said something along the lines of, 'Ma'am, may I wish you a very happy birthday, and many more of them.'

I suspect the Queen was not totally convinced by this flattery, but she still must have been surprised by the very audible pronouncement from the rotund racehorse trainer Jeremy Tree, who had always had something of a rivalry with Guy, of 'Oily fucker'.

This, of course, threw everyone there slightly off their game, and embarrassed mutterings ensued. Once again, the Queen must have left Badminton with some doubts about the lifestyle of its occupants and their friends, although such was her professionalism that nobody could be sure what she was thinking.

We have maintained the tradition of having a member of the Royal Family presenting the prizes. In recent years Princess Anne, who competed in the 1976 equestrian Olympics, and also won the Burghley Horse Trials in 1971, has fulfilled this duty and I have sat next to her at lunch, hosting her on a number of occasions. She is very easy company, with her down-to-earth but slightly unusual wit, and one can have nothing but admiration for her astonishing work ethic.

Perhaps the most significant Horse Trials was the most recent, because the Coronation of King Charles took place on the same weekend. This was initially a cause for much panic, as we wondered if anyone would attend, but the provision of a bank holiday on the Monday meant that we could move the main days back to the Sunday and Monday after it, and the loyal Badminton crowd seemed to come in their normal numbers.

In 1953, ten thousand people were invited to the Queen's Coronation, including all the peers of the realm. Master and Mary, as close friends (and in Mary's case, a relation) of the Royal Family, both attended, with Master dressed in full ducal robes.

King Charles's Coronation was quite rightly slimmed down for the modern era, possibly luckily for me as I had no idea where the ducal cape that Master had worn was, and an expensive tailor's bill was in prospect if we had been asked. I had, however, been strangely moved by the Queen's death and can recall exactly where I was when I heard the news, as I drove back from the golf course. From that day up until the funeral the flag on top of Badminton House flew at half-mast. This was, of course, a few months after her platinum jubilee for which we had organised a street party in the village, and also lit one of the sea of bonfires that went right across the country to celebrate the occasion.

As someone who has also come into his position by accident of birth, I sometimes reflect how lucky I am to enjoy all the benefits of that inheritance without suffering the gaze of the public eye that all members of the Royal Family are permanently under. Even for those Royals who are out of favour, this endless scrutiny can perhaps excuse some elements of their behaviour.

Day-to-day working life at Badminton is varied, and Georgia and I could not do it without the team of two butlers, chef, housekeeper, dailies and gardeners with whom we work very closely. This house is too big for us to run on our own, and a good deal of our work involves entertaining large groups – whether it be for the Horse Trials or other commercial activities connected to the house. We are very proud of our staff, and we get on well with them. They, in turn, seem to enjoy the whole spirit of life at a twenty-first-century Badminton.

Living and working here means that in some ways none of us are ever off the clock. For our staff, although some days can be relatively quiet, this is when they – and we – must think about the maintenance of Badminton and the constant round of refurbishment and restoration that plagues all houses of this size and age. There's a rolling programme of pictures that need cleaning, furniture to be mended and cracks in ceilings that wink at us from above and will at some stage have to be attended to; when we first moved into the house, Viv, our housekeeper, told Georgia not to look up for fear of what she might see.

At busy times it is like putting on a production, whether it is a garden opening – when the air is humming with leaf blowers and hedge trimmers – or a large evening event – when Georgia sits in the kitchen for hours in advance going through recipe books, menus and timetables with the team. We discuss room lists and placement (I like to think of myself as a bit of an expert on this subject), and I meet with Charlie, the head butler, to choose the wine. Flowers, fruit and vegetables are picked, whenever possible, from our walled garden, and Georgia goes on what she calls her 'rounds', checking the rooms to make sure guests will have everything they need. Neither of us really considered that we would end up in 'hospitality', but we have both always liked giving people a good time, and entertaining at Badminton is really just an extension of that.

There is desk work too – estate meetings tend to generate a fair amount of paperwork – and Georgia also continues to write magazine articles and teach undergraduates one day a week. On a quiet day we will both go to our desks in our respective studies after breakfast and not meet again until lunch, which is prepared by Alan the chef and is often an opportunity for us to try out new recipes.

Life for me now is probably busier than it has ever been,

and in some ways I feel that my past experiences all feed into this time, when I am encountering new people from all walks of life through the business and social activities at Badminton. A weekend in June could easily include hosting the Beaufort Hunt Hound Puppy Show, Georgia's garden opening and a night or two at the Glastonbury Festival. Sometimes the timetable of combining these events requires Superman's speed of costume change, although fortunately, considering my renowned clumsiness, I am not required to do this in a telephone box.

Greeting the crowd from the stage when The Listening Device supported
The Who at a concert in the park at Badminton.

Welcome to the Machine

IT IS NOW a few years since I began this memoir. I am still sitting at the desk, which is appallingly untidy, but in my own head there is an order to it all. There are very disordered piles of books and CDs, as well as over fifty volumes of my diaries and the two spaniels sprawled on the sofa. Above all, there is a huge television that begs to be turned on, especially when Test match cricket or National Hunt racing is in the offing.

Television is still one of my great loves and in some ways my friends Giles Wood and his partner Mary Killen have my dream job as part of the cast of the surprise hit TV show, *Gogglebox*, although when I was invited to be on the celebrity version, I politely declined. When I used to stay at Drynachan, Scotland, with Emma and Liza Campbell, Giles and Mary were often guests too. Giles always had a particularly unusual sense of humour in that he could make the most mundane of remarks, such as, 'It's filling up nicely in here' or 'There's a good class of person here tonight', and leave me uncertain whether he was indulging in deliberately clichéd humour or simply making a rather dull observation. This was made even more confusing by his ability to keep a totally deadpan face as he made the remark, and I can remember him using this skill at Drynachan when he summoned me outside around midnight with a conspiratorial, 'Come and listen to this.' He placed his ear against the bark of a substantial tree in the garden, with a look of extreme concentration etched on his face. I did the same but couldn't hear anything, but he had sounded so earnest in making the request that I almost expected to. I didn't realise the extent of his fame until I witnessed him and Mary being mobbed when I happened to be on the same plane a few years ago.

I continue to play in The Listening Device and in recent times we have performed in venues both near Badminton and in London. In the summer of 2023 a rather more exciting opportunity presented itself as we agreed terms with some music promoters about them putting on a concert featuring The Who in the park. I gently suggested to them that my band might be a suitable support act and we found ourselves playing on a stage at least as big as the Pyramid Stage at Glastonbury in front of several thousand people. Although I say it myself, I think we performed very well, although I'm not sure everyone understood the genuine nature of my hospitality when I began our set with the words, 'Welcome to Badminton.'

Badminton remains a regular destination for our families. Monster comes down from London most weekends and is an asset to any house party with her forensic but sometimes unusual analysis of all aspects of news. Eddie and Johnson both have houses in the village and often come to meals here, providing some splendid shafts of eccentricity, and Johnson also brings his DJ skills to take a party late into the night.

The next generation are also very much in evidence. Bobby and Bella both have houses in the village, while Xan and my various nieces and nephews, as well as all members of Georgia's family, also come to stay. Bobby married Lucy Yorke-Long in August 2019 and they exhibited astounding fertility in producing my first grandchild, Henry, some nine months later: the consensus is that he is the most charming boy. They had a second daughter, Lara, in 2023. In some ways I feel that I am too young to have grandchildren, but, as some of my contemporaries have now reached the great-grandchild stage, I suppose I am being over-optimistic about my youthfulness.

Bella is ever the restless traveller and is gradually building up a business combining taking clients on trips to far-off lands with wellness coaching, while Xan is in the process of qualifying as a psychotherapist – a concept I find mildly alarming, akin to the Major in *Fawlty Towers* when he urgently whispered to a bemused Basil, 'Fawlty, there's a psychiatrist in the hotel.' The psychiatrist, at the end of the episode, concludes concerning Basil and goings-on at the hotel: 'There's enough material here for an entire conference' – a conclusion that perhaps might also be drawn by some of the more serious-minded visitors to Badminton.

I am lucky to have, in Bobby, an heir who I trust to take on the responsibilities of Badminton. This, of course, is not always the case with estates. Sunny Marlborough started a televised interview about the Blenheim Estate with the words, 'We've had some good 'uns and we've had some bad 'uns.' Bobby has the advantage of a background in finance and is more astute than me about money and attends most meetings with me. Perhaps the best advice I can give him is that, on occasion, some decisions have to be taken on a basis that is not just related to the balance sheet.

Recent years have proved tumultuous, global uncertainties wrought by Covid and the war in Ukraine. Personally, they have thrown into relief how lucky I am. Had the limitations of lockdown descended at any other stage of my life they would have driven me stark staring mad. As I enter my eighth decade, I am still awash with enthusiasm for all that life has to offer.

Coming late in life to my responsibilities, I realise how important it is that a house like Badminton is kept alive with people and activities, both private and commercial. Georgia and I love to fill it with our friends and family, and we recognise our good fortune in being able to enjoy our life and work together. When we are not entertaining, we retreat to three rooms, where we happily eat our dinner in front of a huge television. The first night we spent alone in the house I discovered that the Great Staircase has acoustics to match that of Abbey Road studios. So occasionally, as I am making my way to bed, I belt out a few lines of a song and I listen to them echo up the three floors lined with portraits of all those who lived here before me.

PATH TO REDEMPTION
The Listening Device
Reimagined

I have played with the prog rock band The Listening Device for over twenty years. Our most recent album is *Path to Redemption,* which is a compilation of our best songs from previous albums. It is available on Spotify and iTunes.

Acknowledgements

I am grateful to Sam Carter and Hannah Bourne-Taylor for their editorial guidance. At Hodder & Stoughton I would like to thank Tom Perrin, Alara Delfosse and Christian Duck. And thanks to Emma Dalrymple too, for typing endless redrafts. Most of all I am grateful to all my family and friends for providing the treasure trove of eccentricity that fills this book.

Picture credits